employability
skills

employability skills

skills

How to stand out from the crowd in the graduate job market

Frances Trought

Prentice Hall
is an imprint of

Harlow, England • London • New York • Boston • San Francisco • Toronto • Sydney • Singapore • Hong Kong
Tokyo • Seoul • Taipei • New Delhi • Cape Town • Madrid • Mexico City • Amsterdam • Munich • Paris • Milan

PEARSON EDUCATION LIMITED
Edinburgh Gate
Harlow CM20 2JE
Tel: +44 (0)1279 623623
Fax: +44 (0)1279 431059
Website: www.pearson.com/uk

First published in Great Britain in 2012

ISBN: 978-0-273-74993-6

British Library Cataloguing-in-Publication Data
A catalogue record for this book is available from the British Library

Library of Congress Cataloging-in-Publication Data
A catalog record for this book is available from the Library of Congress

Typeset in 10pt Plantin by 3
Printed and bound in Great Britain by Henry Ling Ltd, Dorchester, Dorset

To my children, Jorrell, Melodie and Symphonie, and to my excellent support network: Shirley Barrow, Aissata Edmondson, Helen George, Karen St Jean-Kufuor, Bronwyn Murphy, Carol Rene, Lee Rose, Amanda Trought and Robert Trought.

Contents

Foreword

Once upon a time, a person left education and got a 'job', which for university leavers was finessed as 'employment'. University leavers were not unique in aspiring to 'careers' – in law or architecture or teaching and so on.

And, for many – but by no means all – graduates, a career was singular and often with one organisation from graduation to (early) retirement. But the changing nature of the UK economy, and the upheavals of the 1980s and 1990s, led to the emergence of 'portfolio careers': one might start as a journalist, spend some time self-employed, re-train as a teacher, develop an IT interest on the side and become a programmer, have two part-time jobs rather than one full-time one, and so on. Possibly never formally retire fully, just wind down.

Consequently, careers professionals started to engage with the underlying issue: employability. Jobs come and go, careers flourish or flounder, but a person's basic employability is the rock upon which the next job/career can be built. What does a person need to allow him or her to succeed and prosper in the 21st-century economy in general, and jobs market in particular? What skills and attributes, taught and learned, acquired and innate, would need to be identified and displayed?

Employability is a simple word: at root, the ability to be employable. But millions of words have been written, and models constructed, and processes invented and refined to teach employability, to identify employability and to benefit from employability.

My personal take on all this is as follows: the underpinning of all employability is the work ethic. Without it, all that follows is merely window-dressing. And, of course, the work ethic is not a synonym for workaholic: it means industrious and hard-working, reliable and conscientious.

Next is communication – speech, writing and personal appearance (body language), both as an individual and as part of a team. Poor formal speech, txt wrtg and weak personal hygiene factors put you on the back foot before you even begin.

Also, the ability to gather information, analyse it, synthesise it and then apply it is a vital skill. Finally, the ability to learn new skills (and teach others) through formal and informal continuous professional development (CPD) is essential: like a shark, as soon as you stop moving forward, you drown.

All of these skills and abilities can be learnt: none is beyond anybody's reach. It is as often about attitude as it is ability, and attitudes can be refined through practise and hard work.

You may well have noticed that employability does not demand a formal qualification. True, one cannot be a lawyer or a physicist without either a qualification or a degree or both, but the lawyers and physicists who languish in un- or under-employment are probably not displaying the underpinning employability traits outlined above.

So the message is clear: a degree is often necessary, but rarely sufficient. Jobs are for today, careers are for the immediate future, but employability is for ever. And employability can be learnt, honed and practised. Oh, and it is never finished.

Mike Hill
CEO, Higher Education Careers Services Unit and Graduate Prospects

About the author

Frances Trought has been a lecturer for the past nine years at London South Bank University (LSBU) and one of the key aspects she has observed is the fact that a degree is just one piece of the puzzle for students' success. There are so many factors at play that lecturers can no longer just focus on their area of specialism. Employability is a key issue that affects the success of all students. The graduate market is becoming increasingly competitive, and students need to understand the employability skills valued by graduate recruiters. To this effect she has run several employability events including 'I Brand: Creating Your Individual Brand', featuring Tim Campbell, the Apprentice winner, and 'Enhancing your Employability Beyond Your Degree: Meet Levi Roots and Discover the Ingredients for Success' with Levi Roots, entrepreneur, and Gary Argent, Association of Graduate Recruiters. The events encourage students to explore their employability while at university. Frances is also project manager for the LSBU Employability Award.

Author's acknowledgements

A big thank you to Katy Robinson, Dawn Phillips and Steve Temblett for embarking on this journey with me from start to finish.

Thank you to all the graduates who supplied their experiences to enable the book to give practical advice to current students.

Thank you to all the organisations and individuals below who have provided valuable advice and examples.

- Helen Alkin, Recruitment Manager, Marks and Spencer plc
- Gary Argent, Business Operations Manager, Association of Graduate Recruiters
- Martin Birchall, High Fliers Research Ltd
- Femi Bola, Director of Employability, University of East London
- Dr David Bozward, Director of Flying Start, National Council for Graduate Entrepreneurship
- Lizzie Brock, Rate My Placement
- Jon Brookstein, Head of Sport Development, British Universities & Colleges Sport
- Rupert Emson, Managing Director, Vero Screening Ltd
- Beckie Fish, Graduate Recruitment Advisor, Sainsbury's plc
- Andrew Grimley, Development and Communications Director, Young Enterprise Scheme (YES)

- Mark Hamilton, KPMG
- Mike Hill, CEO, Higher Education Careers Services Unit and Graduate Prospects
- Jim Ineson, Executive Director, Students In Free Enterprise (SIFE)
- Simon Jenkinson, Deputy Operations Director, Do-it.org
- Richard Kuti, Students' Union President, London South Bank University
- Emma Maguire, The Duke of Edinburgh's Award
- Raphael Mokades, Managing Director, Rare Recruitment
- Aaron Porter, President of the National Union of Students
- Andrew Powesland, Academy Director, London South Bank University
- Carol Rene, *The Students' Guide to Networking*
- SHL People Performance
- Andrew Scherer, Inspiring Interns
- Mike Southon, keynote speaker, best-selling business author and entrepreneur mentor
- Claire Thomas, Graduate Marketing Manager, Centrica.

Publisher's acknowledgements

We are grateful to the following for permission to reproduce copyright material:

Figures

Figure on page 4 adapted from 'Ready to grow: Business priorities for education and skills: Education and Skills Survey 2010', http://www.cbi.org.uk/pdf/20100501-cbi-education-and-skills-survey-2010. pdf (c) CBI 2010; Figures 2.1, 2.2, 2.3, 2.4, 2.5 and the figure on page 68 adapted from The Graduate Market in 2011, www.highfliers.co.uk/down load/GMReport11.pdf © High Fliers Research Limited 2011.

Tables

Table on page 8 from Peacock, L., (2010) 'Best and worst universities for graduate jobs', The Telegraph, 29 July, http://www.telegraph.co.uk/finance/jobs/8138447/Best-and-worst-universities-for-graduate-jobs.html, copyright ©Telegraph Media Group Limited; Table 2.1 adapted from The Graduate Market in 2011, www.highfliers.co.uk/download/GMReport11. pdf © High Fliers Research Limited 2011.

In some instances we have been unable to trace the owners of copyright material, and we would appreciate any information that would enable us to do so.

Introduction

Every year 300,000 students in the UK graduate with a degree: what makes you stand out?

Whether you are studying for an English, history, business or engineering degree, the one thing you will all have in common is the fact that you all need to know how to market yourself. If your goal is to secure employment at the end of your degree or to start your own business, you will need to be able to convince a potential employer or invester that you are the perfect candidate. This is essential whether you wish to work in the private, public, third sector or become self-employed. Regardless of your field, there will always be competition and the need to stand out!

Marketing and graduate development

Marketing is often seen as a business-related activity, but it is essential to every successful graduate. While at university you are developing your own individual brand. When employability is viewed in its crudest form, we are all products attempting to sell our skills in the graduate marketplace. Consider the definition of a product as:

'Anything that can be offered to a market for attention, acquisition, use or consumption that might satisfy a want or need. It includes physical objects, services, persons, places, organisations and ideas.'

(Kotler et al., 2008)

If we place this in the context of employability, the market would be the graduate employment market and the skills we seek to develop throughout our degrees would represent 'anything that can be offered to a market' and we would hope that these skills would 'satisfy a want or need' of a potential employer.

As a result, strong analogies can be drawn between the development of a product and the development of graduates. The skills developed throughout a degree can be seen as the product features, the elements by which you seek to differentiate yourself from the competition – the other graduates in the marketplace.

If this analogy is extended and the marketing mix is considered, further correlations can be seen. The marketing mix is 'the set of controllable tactical marketing tools – product, price, place and promotion – that the firm blends to produce the response it wants in the target market'. (Kotler et al., 2008, p. 49). The four 'P's (product, price, promotion and place) are used by firms and graduates to bring about their desired outcomes – recruiting the best graduates and gaining employment respectively. If we review all of these elements in this context, strong correlations can be drawn.

By definition, price relates to 'the amount of money charged for a product or service. More broadly, price is the sum of all values that consumers exchange for the benefits of having or using a product or service' (Kotler et al., 2008).

Salary is representative of price as it relates to the amount an employer is willing to pay for graduate services. As with price, salary is influenced by supply and demand and correlations can be drawn between surpluses and shortages in the marketplace dependent upon disciplines. Competition also affects price and graduate recruiters will vary their price in order to make their offer attractive.

Salary, just like price, is influenced by the value a customer, in this case a graduate recruiter, attributes to acquiring new graduates. How important do companies see the acquisition of graduates to the development of their business, and how much can they afford to pay?

Promotion in essence relates to how the value/benefit of a product is communicated to the target audience – in this instance, the way a graduate promotes his or her skills by the use of curriculum vitae, application forms, interviews and online profiles. Do not forget that graduate recruiters also want to recruit the best and so, in turn, adopt a promotion strategy in order to make their offer attractive to graduates by attending graduate recruitment fairs, advertising their graduate schemes and inviting students to career open days.

Place, as with product, relates to the distribution and the availability of the product. When looking for employment you will determine how far you are willing to travel and the location within which you are prepared to work. Graduate recruiters also distribute graduates throughout their organisation both locally and globally, representing a wide distribution network.

The Career Life Cycle

The Product Life Cycle (PLC), charts the progress of a 'product's sales and profits over its lifetime' (Kotler et al., 2008). This model can also be modified to chart the development of a career. In the figure below, the PLC has been modified to represent the various stages of your career. At each stage, just as with a product, a strategy needs to be devised in order to sustain a positive result through continued career development represented by promotion, increase in salary or responsibility.

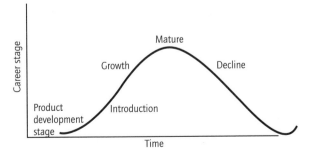

The Career Life Cycle: an adaptation of the Product Life Cycle

The product development stage represents the time that you attend university and develop your skills prior to launching your product into the graduate market. The growth period represents the continued development of your career. It is at the mature stage that you have to make important career decisions in order to keep your career moving upwards. Often companies in the mature phase will release an updated product with additional features to boost sales. At this stage the market has developed either due to the introduction of new technology or new processes and you have to update your skills or risk your skill set becoming outdated. To update skills students will often re-enter higher education at this stage to study for additional qualifications, either a Masters degree or professional qualifications. Others may return to education as a mature student to gain their first degree in order to enhance their career development. The decline phase represents a shift in the market and highlights the fact that your skill set is not aligned with the job market; in many cases, this will result in redundancy. This can often kick-start the Career Life Cycle, forcing a return to the product development stage.

? brilliant question

What stage are you in your Career Life Cycle? Are you still developing your product or returning to education to enhance your product or, following redundancy, seeking to kick-start your career in a new direction?

Due to the increasingly competitive graduate market, and the increasing number of graduates in the marketplace, it has become imperative that graduates engage with the marketing of their skills in order to succeed. Employers can no longer differentiate between candidates based solely on their degree. You now have to consider what else you have to offer a potential employer.

As stated by McNair (2003), graduate employability has increased in importance 'because of the changing nature of the graduate labour market, mass participation in HE, pressures on student finance, competition to recruit students and expectations of students, employers, parents and government (expressed in quality audits and league tables)'.

What do we mean when we talk about employability?

Mantze York defines employability as:

'a set of achievements – skills, understanding and personal attributes – that makes graduates more likely to gain employment and be successful in their chosen occupations, which benefits themselves, the workforce, the community and the economy'

(Yorke, 2006a)

Carl Gilleard, Chief Executive of the Association of Graduate Recruiters states:

'21st-century graduates need to demonstrate to employers that they can "hit the ground running". In addition to working hard to gain a good degree, students should engage in extra-curricular activities and obtain work experience in order to develop skills that will make them better prepared for the world of work.'

The CBI defines employability as 'a set of attributes, skills and knowledge that all labour market participants should possess to ensure they have the capability of being effective in the workplace – to the benefit of themselves, their employer and the wider community' (CBI, 2009).

The CBI builds on this definition and identifies a set of employability skills, including:

- self-management
- team-working
- communication and literacy
- application of numeracy

- business and customer awareness
- application of Information Technology (IT)
- problem-solving
- positive attitude
- entrepreneurship/enterprise

Source: adapted from CBI, 2009

The I Brand Employability Model (right) incorporates these skills but recognises the importance of an individual's network, experience, enterprise and marketing skills. How many times have you heard about a friend getting a brilliant opportunity purely because of who they know? Sure, you will need to be able to perform once you are in the role, but sometimes having a valuable network is just as important as your skill set. The currency of experience is priceless when looking for a position. Repeatedly you will be asked by employers, 'Do you have any experience?' Often you can find yourself caught in a cycle whereby you can't get a job because you don't have any experience, but you can't get any experience because you don't have a job!

The elements of the I Brand model will be discussed in further detail in Chapter 5. Essentially you are building your own individual brand to increase your employability – a brand being defined as 'a name ... that identifies the maker of the product' (Kotler, et al., 2008, p. 511). I Brand encourages you to develop your own skills to make you stand out; to communicate your brilliance to potential employers. From day one at university you need to think about how you will complete your course, but also how you will become a successful graduate. The difference is that being a successful graduate is not merely limited to gaining your degree but also includes developing additional skills that make you more marketable and as a result increase your employability. The definitions of

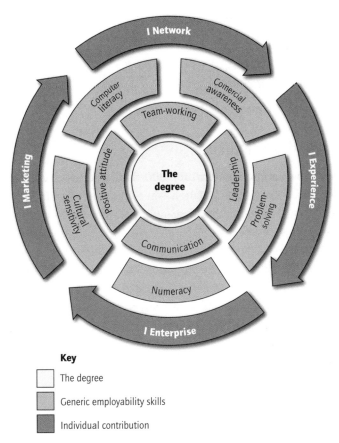

Key

☐ The degree

☐ Generic employability skills

☐ Individual contribution

I Brand Employability Model

employability reference the development of skills and attributes that cannot be developed overnight. To attain these skills graduates cannot leave it to chance or leave to the day before graduation. Students often believe that graduation is far away, but the three or four years will pass very quickly. Students need to actively engage with their career development to ensure that upon graduation they have developed a brand employers want to buy.

 question

If your name was a brand, what would it stand for? What is your unique selling point (USP)? Reliability? Honesty? Trustworthiness?

The graduate market

Every year approximately 300,000 UK graduates enter the job market, creating a situation where the demand for jobs far outstrips the supply. Graduate recruiters have increased their expectations of graduate hires, continually raising the stakes. In the summer of 2010, 78 per cent of graduate employers required a 2:1 degree or above (AGR, 2010). Despite the recession and the increasing doom and gloom, 2009/2010 saw a slight increase in the number of graduate vacancies, with the year ending with a 8.9 per cent increase (AGR, 2011a).

How to use this book

This book is aimed at students studying at levels 4 and 5 of the National Qualifications Framework (first- and second-year university students) to encourage them to get involved in university and all that it offers. The exercises and information are still applicable to final-year and Masters students. The book provides a range of exercises focused on self-exploration and self-development, in order to increase students' marketing potential. Students are encouraged to evaluate their current skills and devise an action plan to develop additional skills while at university through extra-curricular activity. Chapters 2, 3, 4 and 5 provide an overview of the job market and how to navigate your way through it. Students are presented with a number of options to gain work experience while at university and also research alternative avenues to enter your first-choice career.

Chapter 6, Communicating your Brilliance, focuses on how you can market your skills to potential employers and highlights the dos and don'ts of applying for jobs. Chapter 7 encourages students to recognise that this is not a one-off process but, to have a truly Brilliant future, students need to continually review their skill sets to ensure they remain employable.

CHAPTER 1

Not just a degree, a Brilliant degree

'A degree alone is not enough. Employers … value skills such as communication, team-working and problem-solving. Job applicants who can demonstrate that they have developed these skills will have a real advantage'

Jones, 2004

I n order to truly benefit from your time at university and leave with more than just a degree, students need to recognise the skills employers value. Generic employability skills are core to all graduates regardless of discipline. Employers have an expectation that when they recruit a graduate, their ability and aptitude to demonstrate employability skills is a foregone conclusion. In many cases a degree is merely the passport for entry; it is the demonstration of employability skills that is used to differentiate candidates. These skills are built into the curriculum and can be further developed through participation in extra-curricular activities. The first step for students is to understand what is meant by employability and the skills valued by employers. The second stage is to recognise these skills within the curriculum and how they can be gained through extra-curricular activities. This chapter highlights the ways in which universities attempt to embed employability into the curriculum, but also how students can take charge of their own development of employability skills utilising extra-curricular activity both on and off campus.

What do employers want?

Employability is a key priority for employers when recruiting graduates. A report entitled 'Future fit: Preparing graduates for the world of work' stated:

'Over three quarters (78 per cent) of the firms who responded to the Confederation of British Industry's 2009 Education and Skills survey

*said it [employability skills] was one of the most important factors
when recruiting graduates, along with a positive attitude (72 per cent)
and relevant work experience/industrial placement (54 per cent).'*

Source: CBI, 2009, p. 11

A degree allows you to enter the arena, but it is students' ability
to develop relevant employability skills that will differentiate
them from the competition and help secure a graduate position.
Students who are able to communicate the relevance of the skills
developed throughout their degree and those developed through
extra-curricular activities to the world of work will be the most
successful. An Education and Skills Survey conducted by the
CBI/EDI in 2010 attempted to gauge how satisfied employers
were with graduates' employability skills.

Despite the overwhelming satisfaction shown by employers, with
all but one skill rating over 50 per cent for 'satisfied' and 'very

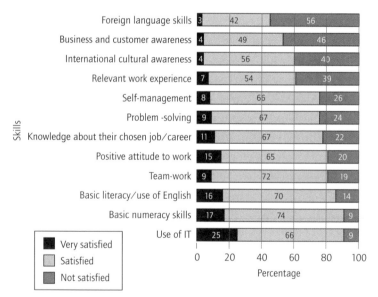

Employer satisfaction with graduates' employability skills
Source: adapted from CBI/EDI, 2010, p. 25

satisfied', the table still presents some alarming concerns. One in ten employers is not satisfied with graduates' basic skills such as numeracy, literacy and IT, which presents an opportunity for significant improvement, especially when these skills are at the heart of academia. The fact that only IT skills can boast a 25 per cent 'very satisfied' rating confirms that graduates need to harness their employability skills prior to graduation. This responsibility rests both with the university and the individual. High on the agenda for areas of improvement are business and customer awareness, where joint satisfaction levels only just surpass 50 per cent, and international cultural awareness and relevant work experience, which currently have satisfaction levels of 60 per cent and 61 per cent respectively. Of even more concern is the fact that regarding skills one would expect to be embedded in the curriculum, i.e. self-management, problem-solving, team-work, 1 in 5 employers is not satisfied.

Two-thirds of employers felt 'gaining practical work experience' was invaluable to graduates in order to develop their employability skills. This statement is reinforced by the findings of 'The graduate market in 2011' (High Fliers Research, 2011, p. 29), which states:

'Many recruiters commented that irrespective of the academic results that a graduate had achieved, it would be very hard for an applicant to demonstrate the skills and competencies that they were looking for if they'd not had any prior work experience.'

The importance and relevance of employability skills will continue to increase and will become the determinant of graduates' success. As stated above, academic results pale into insignificance when compared to students' employability skills.

Why are these skills important?

Regardless of your discipline, career choice or preferred industry sector, these skills underpin your success. Whether you're an arts, engineering or chemistry graduate, you will need to produce

Employability skill	Relevance to the workplace
Team-working	When you join an organisation you will undoubtedly become part of a team, so your ability to work with others and to perform within the group becomes an important skill set. Your ability to participate and add value to your team is essential
Leadership	The ability to demonstrate leadership skills, to take ownership of a task and be able to negotiate, influence and be assertive in your approach to secure a positive outcome. Leadership skills are required by all who have responsibility within an organisation
Positive attitude	Underpinning a positive attitude is viewing the glass as half-full as opposed to half-empty. Positive energy and a willingness to be open to new ideas and alternative solutions will enable you to develop creative solutions to challenges in the workplace
Communication	Communication, both verbal and written, is an essential requirement for graduate roles. The ability to communicate both to internal and external customers is paramount. Accuracy in your written work is a must, and confidence and clarity when speaking in meetings and on the telephone is essential
Problem-solving	The ability to analyse, critically evaluate and formulate a solution are essential skills. Graduates will be expected to be able to demonstrate critical thinking and analytical skills via their academic study or through their work experience
Numeracy	The ability to engage with numbers and support your arguments with hard facts and figures adds to the validity of decisions or proposed solutions. Accuracy and the ability to analyse numerical data is a must
Cultural sensitivity	Organisations rely heavily on their ability to not only attract a diverse workforce, but also to interact on a global scale with diverse audiences. As a result, the need to be culturally aware is highly valued in an international company
Commercial awareness	Understanding the environment within which a business operates will add to your effectiveness, as you will have an understanding of not only the challenges faced by the organisation but also the opportunities presented by the changing landscape
Computer literacy	IT skills underpin all roles and all graduate roles will expect a certain level of proficiency

reports, find solutions to business problems and communicate effectively with customers, management or colleagues. The development of these skills is paramount to your success; they represent the foundation of the skills required to succeed in the workplace. How are these skills used in the work environment? See table, left.

Are universities responsible for the development of employability skills?

The Robbins report (1963) argued that universities were tasked with 'instructing students in skills suitable to play a part in the general division of labour'. This idea was further compounded by the Dearing report (1997, para. 1.1), which placed higher education as central to the 'development of our people, our society, and our economy ... In the next century, the economically successful nations will be those which become learning societies: where all are committed, through effective education and training, to lifelong learning'.

More recently David Willets (2010), UK Minister of State for Universities and Science, called for universities 'to provide public statements on what they do to promote employability, to encourage them to improve the job-readiness of their students and to do better at getting their students into internships, work experience and work'.

All three quotes show a definitive relationship between universities and the development of employability skills. Universities clearly have a role to play in providing and developing a highly skilled workforce, but to what degree do students have to take responsibility for the development of their employability skills? In a position paper on employability, the Association of Graduate Careers Advisory Services (AGCAS, 2011) advised students to 'take responsibility for [their] own employability'.

The table overleaf shows the employment rates of the top five UK universities for graduate job prospects (Peacock, 2010).

The top 5 universities for graduate job prospects	Employment rate (%)
University of Surrey	96.9
Harper Adams University College	96.5
Robert Gordon University	95.9
University of Cambridge	95.2
King's College London	94.6

Source: *The Telegraph*, 29 July 2010

While at university, students will be presented with opportunities to further develop their employability through extra-curricular activities.

Employability in the curriculum – did we cover that on our course?

All too often, where employability is embedded in the curriculum, students do not readily make the connection between their learning and the world of work. This section reviews some of the assessment methods adopted by subject areas to ensure students develop valuable skills required in the workplace.

Other examples of employability in the curriculum are the use of placements, where students are allocated credits for undertaking a work placement, usually for a set duration, typically a year. Many degrees often include the opportunity for study abroad, usually for one semester or term. This can greatly enhance students' cultural awareness, which is a skill desired by international organisations. With all the above, you can provide students with a plethora of opportunities to enhance their employability, but how and if they engage with these opportunities is dependent upon the student. A phrase comes to mind: 'you can lead a horse to water but you can't make it drink'.

Assessment method	Transferable skills
Group assignments	Students are often required to work in teams a group task. Students develop project manaç team-building, negotiation and influencing sk highly relevant to the world of work
Presentations	The ability to develop a well-structured presentation that communicates the key points effectively and efficiently is a valuable skill, useful in a variety of situations beyond a degree
Case-study analysis	Case-study analysis presents a business scenario and requires students to utilise critical thinking, analytical and problem-solving skills not only to identify the key challenges, but also make recommendations drawing on both the internal and external environments faced by the organisation. Case-studies are often used within the selection process to differentiate candidates
Report-writing	Accuracy and clarity in report-writing is a must! Literacy skills are central to your academic studies and for application forms and writing reports or emails in the workplace
Problem-based learning	The ability to resolve problems and provide well-founded solutions is directly transferable to the workplace, where students will be continually presented with challenges
Research	Research skills are applicable to all industries. The ability to collate, synthesise, analyse and clearly present information found can add value to all organisations, whether private, public or third-sector. All industries are reliant upon information to provide insights to current industry dynamics, future trends and possible opportunities and threats in the marketplace
Personal development planning (PDP)	PDP encourages reflection on your strengths and weaknesses and develops self-awareness, which supports continual development and learning
Examinations	Examinations present the opportunity to apply your understanding to scenarios or questions within a time constraint. Many professions utilise professional examinations to test candidates' knowledge and application of the subject matter. An ability to pass examinations is a required skill within the work environment. Examinations are also used as part of the interview process and so have relevance in many work-related situations

Employability and extra-curricular activities – get involved!

University presents students with an opportunity to experience a whole host of new experiences, from running a society to voluntary work, but you have to make the decision to get involved. Often students will say, 'But I don't have time!' My answer to you is *make* time. We all have periods in our days where we think, 'Where did the time go?' Dedicating time to extra-curricular activities is an investment in you! There is so much to be gained that you can't afford to miss out. It is these aspects of your time at university that help you to stand out upon graduation. You will have a wider pool of experiences to talk about than just your academic studies, not to mention your self-development from taking part in these activities. Getting involved in extra-curricular activities also speaks volumes about your character. It shows an employer that you have initiative, energy and lots of get up and go! This chapter will present a range of opportunities that you can get involved with from day one at university.

The students' union

The students' union is an opportunity to develop employability skills while having fun. You can either join an existing society or create your own! A freshers' fair is held at the beginning of the academic year and it is an opportunity for existing societies to showcase to new students, but also to recruit new members. Often students sign up at the freshers' fair but don't become actively involved. Students should seize this opportunity to become active within the society to help organise events and network with students from different courses and various faculties. You can also put into practice many of the skills learnt on your course: event management students could manage, market and budget events, while IT students develop websites and create member databases. The possibilities are endless, but it all starts with your willingness to get involved. The opportunities presented by the students' union are not limited to your university: every university has a union so there are also opportunities to collaborate. You can develop degree-related and self-development skills, which enhance your confidence and make great talking points at interviews. There is no limit to the opportunities presented by being involved in the students' union: the only limiting factor is you!

brilliant tip

Employers are always looking for the candidate who stands out from the rest. Across the country in students' unions and common rooms thousands of students are involved in a variety of activities, including running societies, playing sport, campaigning, supporting other students and helping to run many projects within students' unions. Whether I meet students who are deeply involved or students who are involved in one aspect of student life at university, their skills are evident. Indeed, the NUS has worked with the Confederation of British Industry to catalogue the skills that students develop by engaging in their students' unions as employers value them as employees so much. From learning how to handle budgets, leading groups of students, gaining campaigning skills, building teams, supporting new students and also communicating effectively – by getting involved in your students' union, in something you're passionate about you will become that 'stand out' candidate and have a better time at university because of it.

Aaron Porter, President of the National Union of Students

The majority of societies have a range of either elected or appointed posts: president of the society, treasurer, marketing officer, event co-ordinator. Employers are impressed by students who can demonstrate the skills required to run a society success-fully, as it builds a range of skills.

- Leadership skills
  - You don't have to be the president of a society to develop leadership skills. Taking ownership of a task or role and demonstrating the ability to influence, negotiate for resources and motivate others to achieve a common goal are all examples of leadership qualities. These skills will resonate with an employer as part of an organisation's goal is to identify people, who have the ability to lead/manage a team.
- Project management
  - Whether you are at university or in the workplace, you will always need to have a clear plan of action, as to how you will achieve your goals. The ability to plan, adhere to deadlines, identify key milestones and to succeed are all part of the organisational skills required within the work environment.
- Event management
  - The co-ordination and planning involved in a successful event demonstrates your ability to multitask and strong organisational skills. Event management requires a high level of organisational skills, from liaising with speakers and developing and distributing the marketing communication to negotiating additional resources. The ability to co-ordinate a successful event is an impressive addition to your CV. The busy workplace will always require the ability to multitask, while maintaining standards. Organisational skills and the ability to meet deadlines are musts for successful graduates.
- Budgeting
  - The ability to budget and forecast demonstrates an understanding of how decisions will affect the bottom

line. For instance, understanding how to budget for 1 costs associated with an event and balance these cost: relation to ticket sales to break even or make a profit are valuable skills. All organisations will value these skills, and will especially value your ability to highlight the relationship between decision-making and the impact on costs, as the economy requires all industries to operate efficiently. These skills are directly transferable to all industry sectors.

- Communication
  - Both written and spoken communication can be developed in participation in a society and their value is transferable to the workplace. The ability to write a persuasive email or report (for example, requesting support for the society) or the development of effective marketing materials (for instance, providing members with updates and information) are useful skills. Employers will expect a high standard of literacy and communication skills. You will be required to produce reports, communicate with clients and provide information to other departments in the organisation.

- Networking
  - Networking will help the enterprising student to secure additional resources for their society, engage the services of speakers and professionals for a reduced fee and meet individuals from different backgrounds and interests. Networking is the backbone of all business. The ability to maintain a wide network is useful not only for university but also to identify possible opportunities.

As a result you can develop valuable skills on campus and you can decide how you manage your time in relation to your studies. Joining and becoming active in your union is a great way to build practical examples of your skills for future application forms. The other often-overlooked skill involved in joining a society is your ability to self-manage. Your decisions and actions are all self-directed and speak volumes about your ability to manage and influence others.

brilliant example

My time as a student was very contrasting and memorable. I started off studying in 2006 and had minimal involvement with university, like most of my peers. I would occasionally have a few drinks in the bar but apart from that I was not engaged in any activity til late 2008 in the third year of my four years at university. I was very business-minded and decided that I wanted to start an entrepreneurship society that would help students start up their own business while at university. This grew and as a result I became involved in events planning, project management and public speaking opportunities promoting the society's activities. In essence it was like taking on a part-time job that I was extremely passionate about and, most importantly, I was in control of my time, my contribution and my impact on others. This experience was instrumental in me getting two job offers in completely different fields despite not initially applying for both jobs.

For that reason it's important to get as much work experience as possible while at university, as there are all types of activities to try. I realised that I was part of the small percentage of students who were willing to be proactive outside of my studies, and that made me stand out. An upper second or a first is fantastic; however, without developing your employability your degree may sometimes be in vain.

A business administration graduate

Voluntary work

When I mention voluntary work, often the first response from students is 'I can't afford to work for free'. With increasing student debt and the rising cost of living, no one would expect you to give up paid part-time work, but even if you just volunteer for an hour a week, by the end of the year you would have donated 52 hours of voluntary work. Before deciding to get involved, students should assess their existing commitments and be realistic about the amount of time they have to offer. Volunteers provide valuable support to charities and organisations and so there has to be a certain level of commitment. Complete the following time assessment to review how much time you have available to volunteer. Enter details of your classes, home study, part-time work, any sports or other commitments. This will highlight what time you can devote to volunteering.

	Monday	Tuesday	Wednesday	Thursday	Friday	Saturday	Sunday
9.00							
10.00							
11.00							
12.00							
13.00							
14.00							
15.00							
16.00							
17.00							
18.00							
19.00							

Volunteering provides a wide range of opportunities for students to undertake and develop an array of skills. Organisations recognise that the relationship represents a win–win situation as they benefit from the additional resource that volunteers represent, and students are provided with opportunities for self-development and a chance to experience various career options. The greatest benefit of volunteering is the sense of achievement. By giving even just an hour a week you can make a difference to an individual, a community or an organisation.

brilliant tip

Volunteering isn't just good for the soul; it can also put you on track to improve your career. Volunteering is a way to develop new skills, build your confidence and show future employers you've got drive and initiative. Do-it.org.uk, which is run by the charity YouthNet, has 1.6 million opportunities to choose from across the country so it is a good place to start looking.

Whether you choose to work in the private, voluntary or public sector, volunteering can set you apart from other candidates when applying for jobs. Don't be put off if organisations you are interested in cannot accommodate you; some don't have the resources to manage volunteers, but there are always others to try. Do-it.org.uk has the widest range of available opportunities, but if you prefer to speak to someone directly about opportunities in your area, find your local volunteer centre with Do-it.org.uk's volunteer centre finder. If you want volunteering to help boost your career, think carefully about the skills and experience you need. Don't be afraid to be upfront about this when you apply for opportunities. Volunteering can be a great chance to try different things and, as long as you show commitment to your voluntary work, most organisations will welcome the fact that it could have knock-on benefits for you.

Whatever you want to achieve through volunteering, the basic advice is the same: find a volunteering opportunity that really interests you. You might be volunteering with a big national organisation or a small local one, and it might be the cause that excites you or the specific role, but you will still get much more out of giving your time if it is something you really want to do.

Simon Jenkinson, Deputy Operations Director Do-it.org.uk

From an employer's perspective, a candidate who can demonstrate a willingness to help others and give up their time represents valuable qualities that many organisations would like to see replicated in their employees. Both public- and private-sector organisations have objectives related to corporate social responsibility and often encourage employees to get involved with volunteering initiatives.

The benefits of volunteering are far-reaching for both the volunteer and the beneficiary. Additional examples of volunteering possibilities include the Duke of Edinburgh's Award and Students in Free Enterprise (SIFE).

 **example**

The Duke of Edinburgh's Award, www.dofe.org

The DofE is an award that has three progressive levels: Bronze, Silver and Gold. The aim of the award is to inspire, guide and support young people in their self-development. Students are also presented with opportunities to develop concrete examples of abilities such as leadership skills, team-building, commitment, perseverance and organisational skills.

As stated by a Gold participant: 'The Duke of Edinburgh Award has a good status and currency among employers'.

Students In Free Enterprise (SIFE), www.sifeuk.org

A better world starts with better people – people who have the ability and are willing to put forth the effort to make a meaningful contribution to their communities and the lives of others. SIFE is a unique network of people who answer that call – a global network of business executives, academic leaders and university students sharing the common view that business, practised ethically and responsibly, creates stronger communities and greater opportunities for everyone. Any person enrolled as a graduate or undergraduate student at a university, whether full- or part-time, is eligible to participate in SIFE. Students can be from any academic discipline and in any year of study. Students form a SIFE team and have complete control over how the team is run and what projects they decide to undertake.

Example of a SIFE project: trading futures

This project aims to equip 13–18-year-old students with basic market awareness and personal money management and empower them to pursue higher education and top careers.

Enterprise opportunities

Have you got what it takes to run your own business? University provides an excellent environment to start your own business. Most universities provide training and support for students to explore business ideas, through academic study or extra-curricular activities. Facebook and Dell were both started at university and then expanded upon. Do you have an idea you want to explore? Now is the time to do it as there are experienced advisers willing to provide support.

brilliant tip

The National Council for Graduate Entrepreneurship (NCGE) was formed in 2004 with the aim of raising the profile of entrepreneurship and the option of starting your own business as a career choice among students and graduates. NCGE provides support through workshops, online webinars, business start-up programmes, mentoring and an online support site. The package is aimed at ensuring the student's entrepreneurial journey can be developed both while studying and after graduation. Go to www.mihmentoring.com to find out more.

Dr David Bozward, Director of FlyingStart, National Council for Graduate Entrepreneurship

If you are sitting on a business idea, use these tips from Mike Southon, author of *The Beermat Entrepreneur* (Prentice Hall, 2002) and *This is How Yoodoo It* (Ecademy Press, 2010) to explore your ideas further whilst you are at university.

brilliant tip

Exploring enterprise while at university

1   Develop your network of potential cornerstones – entrepreneurship is about people, not ideas.

2   Find mentors among the academic staff – they will be useful for the rest of your life.

3   Try your new business ideas on your friends at university – if your friends won't buy, then strangers will be even more difficult to persuade.

4   Always look for business opportunities in the academic course that you are studying – it's good to start with something you know.

5   Look for business opportunities in the geographical area where you are studying – local is good!

Mike Southon, keynote speaker, best-selling business author and entrepreneur mentor

Many students use their talents to support themselves during their time at university. Ultimately their goal is not to start their own business, but the attraction is working for themselves, deciding their own rate of pay and their own hours. Review your skill set: do you have a skill that you could use to earn money? This will give you greater flexibility as you will be your own boss. Employers need employees who have an entrepreneurial spirit! To run a business while at university demonstrates to employers your creativity, your initiative and your ability to run a project successfully. Students have given piano lessons, tutored students in maths and English, built websites, etc. Obviously you need to be proficient in your skill first, but it sounds very impressive that you ran your own business while at university!

▶ brilliant example

For years my mum pushed me: 'These piano lessons will come in handy one day. Once you get to grade 8 you can stop'. At university I was looking for a part-time job and I saw an advertisement in the paper for a piano tutor. My mum's words rang in my ears. She laughed when I told her that I was tutoring piano. I tutored students right through my degree. At every interview I went to, the interviewer was always impressed by my ability to manage my own business. Thanks, Mum!

A dentistry graduate

Business challenges present another avenue for exploring enterprise at university. Many universities run replica *Dragon's Den* competitions or business challenges, which allow students to explore their entrepreneurial skills. There are many schemes in operation, so do your research, see what's already running at your university or scout out businesses that offer schemes for you to get involved. A few examples are listed below:

- The npower Energy Challenge and Future Leaders Competitions: www.npower.com/brightergraduates/our-competitions.html
- IBM Universities Business Challenge: www.uk.ubcworldwide.com
- CIMA Global Business Challenge: www.cimaglobal.com/Events-and-cpd-courses/globalbusinesschallenge/

brilliant tip

Young Enterprise Scheme (YES), www.young-enterprise.org.uk

The YES allows students to run their own business, gaining practical experience of the challenges faced by entrepreneurs. Students develop enterprising skills, attitudes and behaviours including:

● creative thinking and problem-solving

● communication and presentation skills

● confidence and a can-do attitude

● team-work and leadership

● negotiation and decision-making

● setting goals and time management

● managing risk and responding to change.

Students are supported by business volunteers and the YES network. This is an excellent opportunity to discover if you have what it takes to be an entrepreneur!

Sports

Whether you play basketball, netball, tennis, hockey or football you are developing employability skills. Sport represents an opportunity for students to actively demonstrate their employability skills. As team captain, being the spokesperson for the team or motivating team members are valuable skills on and off the court.

brilliant tip

Employers view participation and achievement in sport as a favourable addition to your CV. Being physically active and taking part in sport helps you develop transferrable skills that can be

▶

applied in the workplace and including your sporting hobbies and any sporting achievements on your CV is a valuable way to market yourself to potential employers.

Stating that you coached the league-winning hockey team at university shows employers that you have good coaching skills (which can be transferred to non-sports situations). Being a team treasurer is a sure sign you're good with numbers.

Perhaps the most obvious value learned in team sports is being able to work as a team, but in what ways are you a valuable team member? Are you the motivator? Are you the listener? Were you the player to speak up on behalf of your team-mates when you weren't happy with the coach's opinion? Other soft skills learned in sport include co-operation, leadership, tenacity, dedication, respect for others, being a good loser or winner and having a heightened sense of self-awareness in competitive environments.

If you were part of a team during your whole time at university, it shows consistency, adherence to a task and that you can build and sustain relationships with your team members.

Andrew Powesland, Academy Director, Academy of Sport, London
South Bank University

At university, students are encouraged to get involved in sport, as it provides so many opportunities to travel, meet students from other universities and recognition for your success, within university, nationally and internationally. British universities and Colleges Sport provides numerous opportunities for students to represent their universities nationally and internationally. The national leagues and championships, including the World University and European Union Championships, are the perfect addition to your experience at university.

brilliant example

At university I was captain of the netball team. We were like a family;
we supported and encouraged each other on and off the court. The key
element I took from sport is never give up. We would be losing a game and
our positive attitude would help us turn it around. I take a very positive
approach to work, as I believe you can always find a solution. Employers
like this and always comment upon my optimism.

A marketing graduate

Course representatives

You are already on the course, so why not be the course rep? The
name may vary but essentially the role involves you being the
voice of students on the course at academic course management
meetings. Students are encouraged to seek the views and opinions of their fellow students and let the course team know the
issues students are facing. The role can be challenging, especially
when there are significant issues occurring on the course, but it
provides a platform to develop management skills – gathering
and preparing information before the meeting, informing students of your role and willingness to represent them, the ability
to communicate with senior course management and defend
students' needs. The skills developed in being a course representative highlight your ability to network, listen, gather opinions
and communicate at various levels.

brilliant example

I was excited to be elected course representative. There were five of us and
only two places. I prepared a speech, which outlined my interpretation of
the role. As a result I received the most votes. I assured students of their

anonymity and gave them plenty of time to provide me with their views and opinions prior to meetings. I would also make announcements at the end of lectures advising students of the forthcoming course boards and my availability. Now, as a team leader, I adopt the same approach. I give my team opportunities to discuss concerns about senior management decisions and in turn I am the collective voice of my team.

A mechanical engineering graduate

Part-time work

Whether you are serving on a cash till, stacking shelves or waiting tables, you are developing your employability skills. Your experience may not be directly related to your future, but performing well in your role will add value to your CV. Being punctual, your length of service and developing customer service skills are all transferable to your career goals. Employers need reliable employees who value their customers and take pride in their work. References are requested regardless of the industry sector you choose, so a glowing reference from your previous employer will always be welcomed by your future employer.

If you are going to work part-time, be the best that you can be. If there are opportunities to be the employee of the month, team-lead or take on extra responsibility, then seize these opportunities. To show advancement in your part-time job is a demonstration of your commitment, dedication and ability to excel.

> **brilliant** example

I worked for three years during my degree as part of a telesales team. In the beginning, I was just one of many cold-calling potential customers and reading from the script. I was reliable, punctual and after six months I was ▶

promoted to team-lead and after my first year I was analysing the sales statistics and making recommendations as to how we could improve the sales pitch. When I reached my final year the company offered me a full-time position in their new marketing offices in Dubai. I was so tempted, but law was my passion. My advice is to excel at all you do: you never know how it may benefit you in the future!

A law graduate

Not just a degree

Don't be fooled: your grades do matter. Graduating with the best class of degree you can is paramount. Missing assignments or skipping classes will make it harder for you to graduate with a Brilliant degree. Tom Peters' renowned book is entitled *In Search of Excellence* (Profile Books, 2004); no one is searching for mediocrity. Look at it from an employer's perspective: if you had a vacancy wouldn't you want the best student in the class? Therefore monitor your grades; aim for a first-class degree. Often students do not understand how their degree is graded. Make sure you know what percentage of your marks each year count towards your final degree classification. Set goals for each year of study.

Degree classification	Year one	Year two	Year three
% of marks towards final degree classification	E.g. 0% must pass all first-year units	E.g. 20% of total marks	E.g. 80% of final marks
Your degree			

brilliant example

I graduated with a 2:2 and it was a struggle to secure my first graduate position. When I attended graduate recruitment fairs companies only wanted 2:1s or above. It was a real blow to be rejected by so many companies. Luckily I had more to offer having completed two years of volunteering while at university and was also very active in sports. It took 40 applications, 35 rejections. 10 interviews and 9 months of stress to gain my first graduate position.

A business graduate

The same applies for the assessment of each of your units. How many units should you complete each academic year and how is each of those units assessed? To be successful you must know the 'rules of the game'. Complete the table below for your year of study, so you are clear about how each unit will be assessed.

Unit or module	Assessment criteria
Unit 1	
Unit 2	
Unit 3	
Unit 4	
Unit 5	
Unit 6	

🌟 **brilliant** questions and answers

Q Why should students get involved in extra-curricular activities?

A Not only does it look good on your CV but it also gives you a better variety of answers at interview. It also develops skills that can't always be learnt through academia, essential for making you stand out from the crowd, also making you more employable as you have better skills that employers see can be easily transferable into the workplace. Anyone can sit an exam, but not everyone can be social secretary for a rugby club!

Claire Thomas, Graduate Marketing Manager, Centrica

brilliant recap

- 'A degree is not enough. Employers are looking for more than just technical skills and knowledge of a degree discipline' (Digby Jones, former Director-General, CBI, 2004).

- Employability skills are one of the key facts when recruiting graduates.

- A degree allows you to enter the arena, but it is a student's involvement in developing relevant employability skills that will differentiate him or her from the competition and help secure a graduate position.

- Work experience is vital in order to be successful upon graduation.

- There is a definitive relationship between universities and the development of employability skills, but ultimately it is the responsibility of the student.

- The skills developed as a result of completing assessments are directly transferable to the work environment.

- Get involved – don't let opportunities pass you by.

▶

- Don't use lack of time as an excuse – make time: it's your future.

- Is there a society that interests you or do you want to start your own society? Take the time to investigate!

- Volunteering adds value to you and the organisations – even if it's just an hour a week or a one-day team challenge, find out what you can donate.

- Whether you want to start your own business or just develop enterprise skills, there are many opportunities to explore at university.

- Review your role as team player, captain or coach and identify how this translates into the world of work.

- Be your course representative – develop managerial skills while studying for your degree.

- Part-time work can present opportunities to develop your employability but also present career opportunities upon graduation. Make sure you perform to the best of your ability. Don't wait for a sign labelled 'opportunity'.

- Make sure you know how your degree classification is determined and how each of your units is assessed. How can you succeed if you don't know how you are being measured?

CHAPTER 2

The job market

Developing your I Brand is not
an option: it's a prerequisite for
success!

Don't underestimate the challenge of finding a graduate position. The graduate market is highly competitive; the number of graduates in the marketplace far outstrips the number of jobs available. The key fact to remember is there are opportunities and every year companies recruit to their graduate schemes. You just need to be ready to compete. One aspect of your preparation is understanding your industry sector. What are the recruiters in your sector looking for? What issues are they facing with current applications from graduates? What areas of the sector do they see in contraction or expansion? Use this information to ensure that you are developing the right skills. How, though, do you access this information?

What is a graduate scheme?

The majority of top employers will offer a graduate training scheme. This is an opportunity for companies to recruit the best graduate talent into their organisations. Graduates are recruited from a wide range of degree disciplines into a wide range of roles. The purpose of graduate training schemes is to offer students the opportunity to experience various roles within the organisation before deciding upon a specialism.

Companies invest in the training and development of their graduate talent, their leaders of tomorrow. As a result the training presents a range of opportunities and exposure to various departments and individuals, but requires dedication and hard work from graduates. In turn, graduates are rewarded with a competitive salary, career opportunities and a targeted training and development programme.

In order to be successful in gaining a place on a graduate scheme, students need to start their search at least a year before graduation, to ensure they are aware of company deadlines and recruitment procedures. A typical recruitment process will include:

- the completion of an online application form
- a telephone interview
- psychometric testing
- invitation to an assessment centre, including a face-to-face interview.

brilliant tip

The current economic climate means that it is vitally important to consider the complete range of skills that graduate recruiters value. Candidates who can demonstrate a combination of strong academic skills through the achievement of a good degree and the crucial 'softer skills' that are so important in business will always be in demand. Active participation in a well-structured employability award and other activities such as involvement in student societies, part-time/holiday jobs or charity work will help you to develop those soft skills and will give you a wide range of experiences to draw on when you engage with employers. Ultimately this breadth of experience will make you stand out from the crowd and help you to demonstrate what you can bring to their business.

Gary Argent, Business Development Manager, Association of Graduate Recruiters

Overview of the graduate market

The graduate market has become increasingly competitive. Not only are you competing with current graduates but also with graduates who have not found positions in previous years. This situation has been amplified by the recession, but 2010 saw a slight increase (8.9 per cent) in the number of graduate jobs available (AGR, 2011a). Despite this increase, the Association of Graduate Recruiters also noted a significant increase in the number of applications for each graduate position. In 2010, AGR members received an increase in applications for graduate jobs: 'the average now stands at 69 for every vacancy, compared to 49 last year and 31 in 2008' (AGR, 2010). In direct response to increased applications, graduate recruiters have raised the entry stakes, so that '78 per cent of employers now insist on a minimum 2.1 degree' (AGR, 2010).

The graduate market is improving, with a forecast increase of 3.8 per cent upon 2010 recruitment figures (AGR, 2011a). High Fliers Research (2011), in their survey of *The Times* top 100 graduate recruiters, also confirm an increase in the market, stating that in 2011 graduates could expect a 9.4 per cent increase in the number of graduate vacancies. The competition is still as fierce as ever, but you always have to keep in mind that there are positions available and you only need one company, one job! You will be rejected on several occasions, but you need to keep going until you find a company that can see the brilliance in you.

Graduate vacancies

Despite headlines stating that 'up to one in four graduates faces unemployment' (Collins, 2010) there has been an increase in the number of graduate vacancies available. A report entitled 'The graduate market in 2011' (High Fliers Research, 2011), which provides an analysis of the graduate recruitment market in relation to *The Times* top 100 graduate recruiters, identified an increase of

9.4 per cent in graduate vacancies compared to 2010. At the start of the recession there was a significant decrease in the number of vacancies, representing a 17.8 per cent decline in comparison to 2008, but there has been a gradual increase in the number of positions available. Figure 2.1 shows how this has been reflected in the industry/business sectors with a comparison of actual graduates recruited by December 2010 with the projected recruitment targets for 2011. The majority of industries/business sectors are

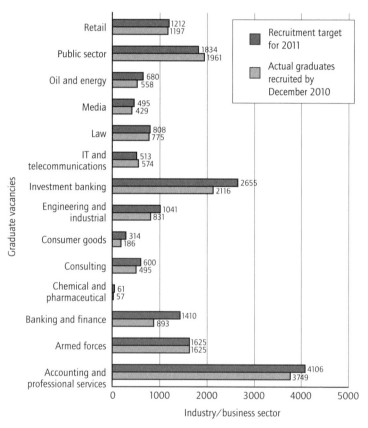

Figure 2.1 Actual graduate recruitment by December 2010 compared with recruitment targets for 2011

Source: based on data from 'The graduate market in 2011' by High Fliers Research

experiencing a growth in their recruitment targets, with banking and finance, investment banking and accounting and professional services experiencing a significant increase. There are slight declines in the public sector, which reflects current trends in the sector.

The majority of these vacancies are based in London, with nine out of ten organisations offering vacancies in London during 2011 (High Fliers Research, 2011), which reflects the high concentration of finance-related vacancies.

Figure 2.2 shows the distribution of graduate vacancies

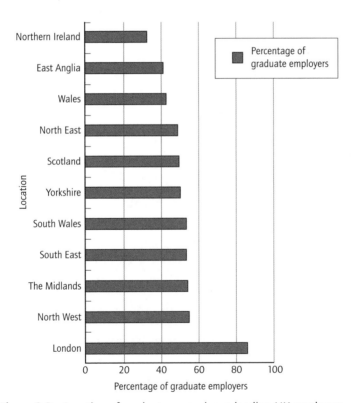

Figure 2.2   Location of graduate vacancies at leading UK employers in 2011

Source: based on data from 'The graduate market in 2011' by High Fliers Research

throughout the UK and Figure 2.3 the types of vacancies available within the top graduate recruiters. Finance-related roles will be the highest recruited area in 2011, but these roles are distributed across various industries and business sectors, highlighting the reliance of organisations on a variety of disciplines in order to compete in the marketplace.

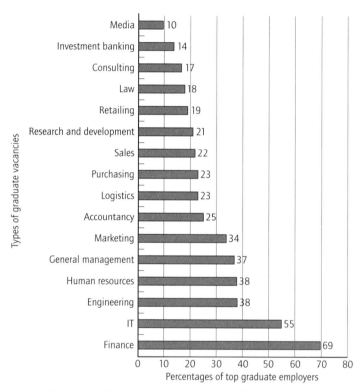

Figure 2.3   Types of graduate vacancies at leading UK employers in 2011

Source: based on data from 'The graduate market in 2011' by High Fliers Research

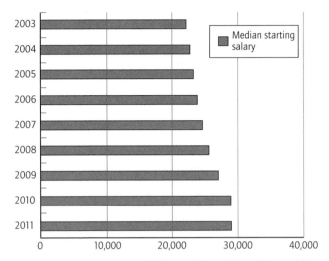

Figure 2.4   How starting salaries for graduates have changed between 2003 and 2011

Source: based on data from 'The graduate market in 2011' by High Fliers Research

Despite fluctuations in the marketplace in relation to the availability of graduate vacancies, salary levels have steadily increased. The initial figures in 2011 show that salaries have been maintained at 2010 levels, but, considering many organisations have either frozen salaries or announced redundancies, this does not seem bad. Figure 2.4 shows the growth in salaries from 2003 to 2011 (High Fliers Research, 2011).

Despite average salaries being between £20,000 and £30,000 there are graduate recruiters who are willing to pay significantly more (see Figures 2.4 and 2.5). In 'The graduate market in 2011' report (High Fliers Research, 2011) seven companies advised that starting salaries would range from £35,000 to £50,000. Graduates can expect salaries to vary considerably depending upon the sector.

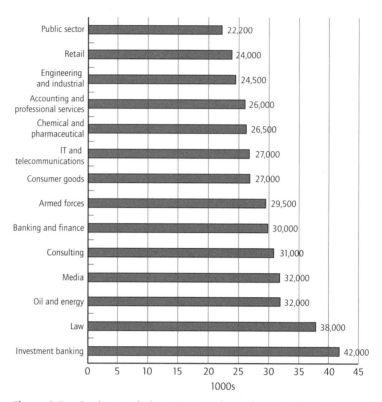

Figure 2.5 Graduate salaries at UK employers in 2011, by sector or industry

Source: based on data from 'The graduate market in 2011' by High Fliers Research

The public sector, with an average starting salary of £22,200, compared to £42,000 in the investment banking sector, reflects the differences between industry sectors.

Work experience

The vacancies in relation to placements and internships emphasise the level of importance placed by employers on students gaining work experience. Employers recognise their role in making these opportunities available, in order to develop students' employability skills (see Figure 2.6 and Table 2.1). Some 63 per cent of the UK's top graduate employers offered 6–12-month industrial placements. By engaging with students at this early stage in their studies, employers are able to identify suitable candidates for their graduate schemes. Internships and placements enable organisations to build relationships with promising students. This is further illustrated in the data as a third of all graduate roles are filled by graduates who have already worked for the employer during their degree.

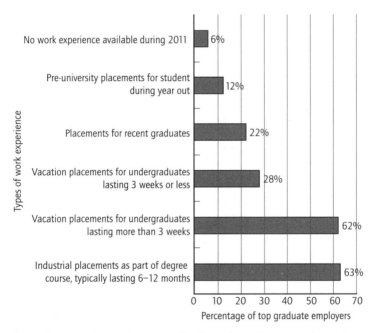

Figure 2.6   Work experience on offer from the UK's top employers in 2010–2011

Source: based on data from 'The graduate market in 2011' by High Fliers Research

In the investment banking sector this figure rises to 53 per cent, more than half of all the graduate vacancies (High Fliers Research 2011; see Figure 2.7). Graduates with no work experience will find it hard to compete as companies want students to be able to provide practical demonstrations of their employability skills.

Table 2.1 Analysis of work experience places 2010–2011

Industry/sector	Total work experience places available 2010–2011
Accounting and professional services	1278
Banking and finance	850
Consulting	180
Consumer goods	201
Engineering and industrial	549
Investment banking	3220
IT and telecommunications	515
Law	825
Media	141
Oil and energy	389
Public sector	333
Retailing	254

Source: based on data from 'The graduate market in 2011' by High Fliers Research

It is important to emphasise the need for work experience. Undertaking an internship or placement is a chance for the company to trial your 'product' and, if the company is impressed, you can receive preference for their graduate schemes. It is therefore essential to gain work experience relevant to a sector of interest.

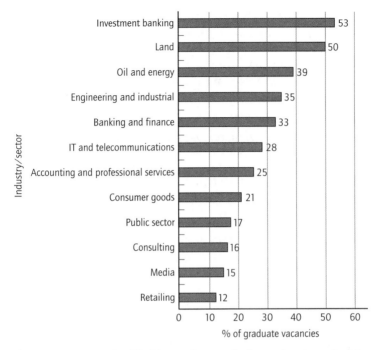

Figure 2.7 Vacancies filled by graduates who have already worked for the employer.

Source: based on data from 'The graduate market in 2011' by High Fliers Research

Diversity and graduate recruitment

Organisations monitor diversity data to ensure that they are receiving applications from a range of candidates and can introduce measures where necessary to increase the diversity of applications and recruits from under-represented groups. The Association of Graduate Recruiters (AGR) found in their 'Graduate recruitment survey 2011 – winter review' (AGR 2011b, p. 24) that for the period 2009–2010, '63 women were recruited for every 100 men'. Women were particularly under-represented in industries such as engineering, construction, IT and telecommunications. As a result, some members were actively trying to increase female recruits, by increasing the level of female staff participation in recruitment fairs and the overall promotion of the graduate scheme.

AGR also found that age was not often monitored in organisations but, when reviewing the age of graduates recruited in 2009–2010, it was found that almost 80 per cent were aged 24 or younger. Some 20 per cent of graduates were aged 25 to 34, which reflects the increasing mature student market (AGR, 2011b, p. 26).

AGR found that in 2009–2010 'one third of graduates recruited from ethnic minorities were Indian' (AGR 2011b, p. 27) with graduates of Chinese origin coming in second at 17.5 per cent. Black and minority ethnic groups are under-represented, so some recruiters increasingly target universities with 'high BME ratios' (AGR, 2011b, p. 24).

In organisations that monitored disability, AGR found that in 2009–2010 'five disabled graduates are estimated to have been recruited for every 100 non-disabled graduates' (AGR, 2011, p. 27).

Challenges facing graduate recruiters

Despite the competitive graduate market, in 2009–2010 26 per cent of AGR members recorded a shortfall in their recruitment targets (AGR, 2011b, p. 26). The main cause was dropout rates; high-quality candidates are often able to secure places on more than one graduate scheme and so are able to choose between employers. This can often leave companies with places on their graduate schemes, where notification is received late in the recruitment process. As a result companies have introduced 'keep warm' strategies to ensure graduates develop an affiliation to the organisation and they become the preferred employer. Although this issue permeates all industries and sectors, the highest shortfalls occur in the accountancy, banking and finance, IT and telecommunications sectors (AGR, 2011b).

The response to the Browne report

The governmental Browne report (2010) entitled 'Securing a sustainable future for higher education in the UK', was published on 12 October 2010. The central aim of the report was to provide recommendations as to the future funding of higher education and the availability and structure of student finance. One of the central recommendations proposed by the report was the cut in funding to higher education institutions and the resulting increase in tuition fees. Students who enter higher education as of 2012 will be faced with tuition fees of up to £9000 per year. This has sparked growing concerns by students, parents and employers about the accessibility of higher education.

As a result a number of companies have developed schemes that will not only pay students' tuition fees but also provide them with paid employment, with starting salaries ranging from £20,000 per annum. The schemes are aimed in particular at school-leavers with A-levels and, although not developed as a direct response to the Browne report, present a valuable way of increasing the accessibility of universities to students.

 **brilliant** example

KPMG School Leavers' Programme

KPMG is one of the 'Big Four' accountancy firms and a major recruiter of young people. Historically, this has been almost entirely made up of graduates, but in 2011 KPMG is launching a new scheme for school leavers that is breaking the mould.

In September 2011, around 100 school leavers will join KPMG on a 6-year programme that will consist of real work experience, an accountancy degree obtained from Durham or Exeter University (or Birmingham University from September 2012) and a professional chartered accountancy qualification. All this while receiving a starting salary of around £20,000

▶

and with all tuition fees (and university accommodation costs) paid by KPMG!

KPMG expects the programme to grow such that, within the next few years, the firm could be taking on around 400 school leavers a year.

Entry requirements are ABB at A level, plus a minimum grade B in maths and English language GCSEs.

One of the main drivers behind the scheme is to broaden access to the accountancy profession and increase the diversity of talent coming in. This means reaching people who might not normally consider accountancy as a career. KPMG wants to ensure that talented young people are not put off pursuing higher education by financial constraints. The planning for this scheme started some time ago and pre-dated the university tuition fees debate – but with fees due to increase, the scheme is doubtless even more attractive.

For students, here is an opportunity to obtain both a degree and a professional qualification that should lead directly to a rewarding (and well-rewarded) career. Add to this the possibility of qualifying without any burden of debt and one can see why the scheme is expected to prove very popular!

Industry/sector

Understanding your industry/sector is paramount! To be successful you need to be aware of the skills needed to compete in your chosen field. There are many ways to develop industry-specific knowledge. Joining a professional body can provide you with regular updates, e-bulletins and networking opportunities with professionals from your chosen industry. The careers service within your university will have specific information on the sector and information on the various roles found within the industry. Your degree will also provide you with a range of industry-specific links from websites to journals to industry speakers. Utilising the alumni is another avenue to not only find out about the industry but also possible opportunities for work experience within their organisation.

Your degree

As mentioned previously, employability is embedded in the curriculum and, in your lectures and assessments, you will be presented with current trends in your industry. Your assignments will include research into changes in the industry, company-specific case studies and future developments impacting the development of the sector. As a result your course is one of the first sources of information about the industry. Reading material will be targeted and provide an insight into industry trends. Reading lists will include industry-sector journals and magazines and relevant websites. Lecturers will often invite industry professionals to deliver lectures on challenges facing the industry and changes in the macro-environment impacting the organisation.

Joining a professional body

All industries have a professional body or network, which can provide an insight into the industry. Becoming a member is not as expensive as you may think. Student membership can range from £20–40. First, find the professional body linked to your career choice. Below is a sample of professional bodies and their membership fees.

Institution of Civil Engineers, www.ice.org.uk

Annual student membership: free

Benefits of membership:

- free access to the online version of *Civil Engineering*
- free access to the online version of *New Civil Engineer*
- question and answer support service
- access to the ICE library

- bi-monthly e-newsletter
- free access to ICE virtual library
- eligible for ICE awards and prizes
- eligibility to join the students and graduate network.

The Writers' Guild, www.writersguild.org.uk

Annual student membership: £20

Benefits of membership:

- support and advice
- weekly e-bulletin
- *UK Writer* magazine (quarterly)
- events featuring established writers and industry specialists
- discounts.

Do some research: find your related professional body as it will keep your industry information and links with industry professionals current!

---

brilliant example

I felt so prepared when I started to look for graduate positions. As a member of the British Computer Society I had kept up to date with the industry news and also attended a number of talks by industry professionals. As a result I had an understanding of the trends and their impact on the current climate. When I went for interviews I could speak quite confidently about the sector and had even formed my own opinions as to forthcoming changes. Interviewers were very impressed with my industry knowledge.

An information technology graduate

Careers service

Don't forget to use the wealth of experience available in your careers service. It will have links with employers and will be able to advise you on the expectations of graduate recruiters. There are also degree-specific graduate industry magazines, which can provide you with additional information. The careers service will also organise a number of graduate and placement fairs, presenting opportunities for you to speak directly with employers.

Alumni network

You are not the first to graduate from your course, so learn from the experiences of others. Use the alumni to field questions about expectations within the graduate market. How hard was it to find a job? What was the interview process? How many jobs did you apply for and when? They are a valuable source of information so either contact your alumni office or speak to lecturers about asking students from previous years to speak to the current cohort.

brilliant example

I owe my first graduate position to an alumnus of my university. He came to talk to our class about his journey after graduation. We were talking after the event and I asked him if we could go for a coffee one day. He became my sounding board. I would ask him to review my CV or for his view on career pathways. When I graduated, he convinced his manager to give me a three-month temporary contract. At the end of that period I was made permanent. Finding out about the industry from someone who graduated from your course is priceless.

A business graduate

Company annual reports and websites

Annual reports and websites will display current information about both the industry and the company. This will be displayed in many formats including downloadable reports or video content. It's a valuable online resource and can provide insight into both the company and the sector. Companies need to attract the brightest and the best, so it is in their interest to provide as much information as possible to attract the right candidates. Review the website of the company you would like to work for. How informative is their website about the company, about the industry? Can you register for any e-bulletins or newsletters?

 **brilliant** recap

- A graduate scheme is an opportunity for companies to recruit the best graduate talent into their organisations.

- Graduates are recruited from a wide range of degree disciplines into a wide range of roles.

- In 2010, there was a slight increase (8.9 per cent) in the number of graduate jobs available.

- The majority of industries/business sectors are experiencing a growth in their recruitment targets, with banking and finance, investment banking and accounting and professional services experiencing a significant increase.

- The majority of these vacancies are based in London, with nine out of ten organisations offering vacancies in London during 2011 (High Fliers Research, 2011).

- Average graduate salaries range from £20,000–30,000, with a number of graduate recruiters willing to pay up to £50,000.

- Companies use internships and placements to trial your 'product' and, if impressed, will aim to offer you a place on their graduate scheme.

- Knowledge is power – make sure you research your industry and leading competitors. Be aware of developing industry challenges and trends.

- Research the professional body associated with your degree: what hints and tips do they offer to students?

- Use all the resources available to you – such as your university's careers service or alumni network.

- Company websites will provide you with an insight to the company and the industry.

- Learn from the experiences of previous graduates on your course. They will be able to give you their experience of the industry and advice on finding your place within it.

CHAPTER 3

Brilliant career planning

If you are going to invest £20,000 in a product, you had better know how to use it!

Planning your career is not an easy task. How do you know if a career is for you just by reading about it? The reality of career planning is you will never know if you have chosen the right career or company until you start working there. Do not ignore established profiles, which have been developed to help identify suitable careers. Your careers service will have a number of tools to help you choose. Every career has clear indicators profiling the types of characters who would enjoy working in that particular role. Your degree will also be an indicator of whether you would enjoy working in roles related to your discipline. Having a good understanding of your goals and aspirations is a key starting point.

Self-assessment

Knowing YOU is the first step to being able to identify a career. You need to understand your likes and dislikes before you can make any decisions. Do you operate well under stress? Do you like working with customers or prefer computers? Do you like to travel or do your personal commitments limit your time away from home? What are your strengths and weaknesses? If you have a good understanding of yourself, then you are better placed to find a career that fits your needs. The careers service will have a range of diagnostic tools for you to use, but there are some simple exercises you can do to understand what's important to you.

 example

Match your goals to your personality

Before you start to think about what you might want to do, you need to know yourself. We're not talking spiritual enlightenment here – what we mean is that you need to know what is really important to you in a job. People often fail to consider these cultural factors and end up unhappy not because the work they are doing fails to interest them, but because of the working hours or the travel or the drinking culture.

So, here's a suggestion. This might take a while and some people find it quite difficult as an exercise, but we strongly suggest that you do it. Take a blank sheet of paper and draw a line down the middle of it. On the left-hand side, write down all the times in your life you can think of when you've been really happy. On the right-hand side, write down all the unhappy occasions.

Now, look at your list. Look for trends. What really makes you happy? Is it working with a group of great people? Is it order, structure and routine? Is it having a fantastic teacher and meaningful learning experiences? Is it material success or the respect of your peers? Then, what makes you unhappy? Is it working too many hours? Being shouted at? Feeling undervalued? Being underpaid? Feeling lonely?

This list is a window into your character. When choosing a career, you need to pick a route that will allow you to be happy. If you hate high-pressured, aggressive environments, then you do not want a career in such an environment. If you value material success above all else, then you shouldn't pick a career that pays badly. It sounds hugely obvious, and it is, but most people never do this and so end up in a career to which they are fundamentally badly suited.

Once you know your own priorities, the next step is to do your research into the companies and industries that interest you. You need to do this fundamental research *before* you go for interview. By far the best way is to use your personal network to talk to someone already working for the firm that interests you and to ask him or her, informally, what it's like to work there. Failing that, you can read brochures, critical websites like Vault (www.vault.com) and attend open days.

Raphael Mokades, author of *Three Steps to Success* (2011)

Personal review

Another means is to conduct a self-assessment by viewing yourself through the eyes of others – a personal review encourages you to gain insight from those you work with on a professional and informal basis. Rate yourself and then ask a minimum of five people, who know you in different capacities, to rate you. Are you as brilliant as you thought? Overleaf are a few suggestions.

Don't take the results to heart, but use them as a means to gain an insight into you. You can also use the results to help you develop an action plan. Often we don't see our strengths or we don't take credit for the things we do, so a personal review helps us to gain another perspective.

brilliant example

The personal review presented a few surprises. My scores were so much lower than the people I asked to review me. They had a much higher opinion of me and identified my strengths and weaknesses. It was a good exercise to see myself through my friends' and colleagues' eyes.

A psychology graduate

Traits and skills valued by employers	1	2	3	4	5
Punctual					
Reliable					
Attention to detail					
Problem-solving					
Communication (oral and written)					
Numerate					
Innovative					
Positive attitude					
Honest					
Meet deadlines					
Accurate					
Can think on your feet					
Organised					
Team player					
Leader					
Negotiator					
Influencer					
Name one strength					
Name one weakness					

Online career-planning resources

www.prospects.ac.uk

Prospects is the 'official graduate careers website' and includes a prospects planner, which serves as a great resource for students to research and read about prospective careers. The tool helps students to recognise their skills and how they translate into potential career paths. There is information specifically related to degree disciplines and useful tools to research career options. The prospects planner is an extensive resource to explore career opportunities based on your skills and ambitions.

brilliant tip

1   How to choose a career that's right for you

Or, what do I want to do when I grow up? To be honest, this is a difficult one as these days people can end up having a number of different careers over their working lives. The best approach is to be open-minded and decide on a particular sector or role that you are interested in and try to look for opportunities, usually at entry level, that get your foot in the door. For example, if you are interested in an accountancy role, try to get a finance-related job in any sector, e.g. administration in the finance section of a construction company, and look for opportunities from within. Consider work in small and medium-sized companies in the sector that you are interested in; don't just consider the industry giants The 'Sunday Times 100 best companies 2010' directory can be useful for this (see http://business.timesonline.co.uk/tol/business/career_and_jobs/best−100−companies/best−100−tables).

2   How to research career opportunities − degree-specific and unrelated

Look on university websites (not just your own university's) and see the destinations of leavers from your programme of study. Talk to people: very often, people stumble on a career, they don't actually plan it. Let them describe their route into their particular career. Go to lectures or meetings at professional bodies and network: you will be surprised at how much information people are prepared to share about their personal journeys when asked. You can always arrange to meet up with them at a later date to find out more about them and their role.

▶

> **3** How to gain experience while studying at university
>
> Take up every opportunity that is available at your university from year one. Join or run a society or club, be a student ambassador, volunteer, be mentored or mentor fellow students at a college or secondary school and try to work every summer – it doesn't matter what you do, just do something! Take on responsibility at your local faith group. All these things will develop skills alongside your studies that employers value and will give you something to talk about at an interview.
>
> Femi Bola, Director of Employability, University of East London

Career goals: blue-sky thinking

In your ideal world, when you graduate, what position do you see yourself in? Now work backwards in order to identify actions to achieve that goal! How do you identify what actions you need to take? Use industry profiles of the skills desired by employers in your chosen career, assess yourself against those skills and identify areas for development. Your personal review will also highlight areas for development.

Regardless of your chosen career path, employers will have generic and specific skill sets they require in their candidates. As a result it is important to understand the criteria against which you will be measured when you graduate. Develop both short- and long-term objectives to ensure your success. Use your own self-assessment, the results of your personal review and employer's requirements for the role you wish to pursue to develop an action plan. These objectives should be SMART:

Specific	What do you want to achieve and by when?
Measurable	How will you know you have achieved your goal?

Achievable	What are the actions or tasks needed to achieve success?
Realistic	Is it likely you can achieve this goal in the timeframe specified?
Timely	Give yourself a deadline

Your goals in your first year may focus on researching the options available to you with your degree discipline. There may be careers you have not considered, as many graduate schemes are not discipline-specific and so you may study psychology but find yourself working in an investment bank. In your first year, one goal may be to explore possible career options and the actions involved in achieving this goal could be researching information about possible careers via the university careers service or developing your generic employability skills through extra-curricular activities. In your second year you may begin to focus on identifying means to gain an internship, noting the deadlines for applications and identifying possible companies. When you reach your final year, your focus will be on identifying graduate schemes and companies you wish to apply to, identifying opportunities to meet with these companies at graduate fairs and open days and networking with previous graduates to learn from their experiences.

It is essential that you set yourself goals and tasks as your time at university will pass very quickly. Use the table overleaf to develop a set of goals for your time at university and the actions to achieve them.

Don't worry if your career goals change. At university you will be exposed to new opportunities and experiences, which will undoubtedly have an impact on you as a person and ultimately your aspirations. This is all part of the development process and will ensure that upon graduation you have a better understanding of YOU!

Overall career goal		
Year 1	Action	Outcome
Goal 1		
Goal 2		
Goal 3		
Year 2		
Goal 1		
Goal 2		
Goal 3		
Year 3		
Goal 1		
Goal 2		
Goal 3		

 **brilliant** recap

- Knowing YOU – your strengths, your weaknesses, your likes and dislikes – is the first step in choosing a career.
- Identify what is important to you – travel, flexibility, money, career progression?
- Research career options by networking with industry professionals or attending employer events, where you can pose your questions to the company directly.

- Network with the alumni of your course to learn from their experiences.

- Use a personal review to identify how you are perceived by others and identify areas for development.

- Create an account on the Prospects website and use the prospects planner to map your career (www.prospects.ac.uk).

- Develop an action plan for your three years of study to ensure you develop the skills required upon graduation.

- Define SMART career goals and the actions needed to achieve them.

CHAPTER 4

Finding a Brilliant job

Invest time in developing
employability skills while studying
so, upon graduation, you can
harvest the return on your
investment

The fact that you are reading this book shows you are interested in improving your chances of employment upon graduation. Finding employment upon graduation is linked to all of the efforts you make while studying to gain valuable employability skills. 'The graduate market in 2011' by High Fliers Research (2011, p. 5) highlighted two important facts.

1 'Nearly **two-thirds of recruiters** warn that graduates who have had no previous work experience at all are **unlikely to be successful** during the selection process and have **little or no chance** of receiving a job offer for their organisations' graduate programmes.'

2 'Although the total number of graduate vacancies is set to increase in 2011, recruiters have confirmed that a **third** of this year's entry-level positions are expected to be filled by graduates who have **already worked for their organisations** – either through industrial placements, vacation work or sponsorships.'

The importance of gaining work experience at university has become a prerequisite for finding employment upon graduation. Job shadowing, internships and placements have become increasingly important. This chapter will look at how to gain work experience while at university and how to gain employment upon graduation.

 **brilliant** tip

What advice would you give students who wish to undertake a placement or internship?

The main thing to bear in mind when finding and choosing an internship is to ensure you will be benefiting from the experience. Do not be afraid to ask what tasks you will be carrying out, who will be in charge of you during your placement, whether or not the company will consider hiring you after the internship and anything else you want to know. Not only will this ensure you don't end up spending time doing something you are not interested in but it will also convey to the employer your enthusiasm and how seriously you are taking the opportunity.

During the internship itself, make sure you volunteer for any projects you're interested in and generally show lots of enthusiasm: it goes a long way. Don't forget, whoever is looking after you has their own work as well, so don't just wait to be told what to do – ask for tasks and make yourself indispensable.

Andrew Scherer, Marketing Manager, Inspiring Interns, and author of *Brilliant Intern*

Types of work experience available

There are many opportunities to undertake work experience while at university. Some are competitive to secure, but the opportunities do exist. Opportunities vary depending upon your level of study. To the right is a list of various types of work experience offered by companies.

Job shadow	Job shadowing is often unpaid, but provides an opportunity to observe a professional at work in his or her work setting. It enables you to gain an insight into the daily tasks and responsibilities involved in a particular role. It also provides a valuable opportunity to pose questions about your career choices and decide whether or not this really is the career for you. Job shadowing can be undertaken in any year of study and used to explore various career options
Internships	Internships can vary in length but are often for a fixed period ranging from 3 to 12 weeks and take place during the Easter or summer holiday. During an internship students will gain a valuable insight into the culture of the organisation, the specifics of the role and, more importantly, can form a view as to whether they are suited to the role or not. Students will be allocated to a supervisor who will assign them a range of tasks and projects. Internships also provide an opportunity to network within the organisation, which can prove very useful in the future
Placements	Placements provide students with a rotation to various departments within the organisation. Companies often target students in their penultimate year of study or those who have recently graduated. Placements are longer in duration and often last for 6–12 months. Students can undertake a placement as part of their course or during a gap year. Placements often form the basis of the final-year dissertation, providing students with an opportunity to research a real issue faced by an organisation or industry. Students can gain a valuable insight into the company, build a useful network and also review their career options as a result of undertaking the placement. If your placement is successful, the company may also invite you to join the company following graduation!

brilliant example

What is an internship and how can it increase students' employability?

An internship is a temporary arrangement between an employer and a student or graduate where the company will host the student for a designated period, usually three to six months. An internship differs from work experience as it usually takes place over a longer period and has greater focus on active participation from the intern, rather than simply shadowing.

▶

Often the intern will work on a specific project or be allocated to a team. Although they are likely to undertake meaningful tasks, this will be under close supervision and guidance from a designated mentor and aims to develop the intern's knowledge of a particular job or industry.

A good internship will help hone the transferable skills you learn at university, develop new commercial ability and allow you to build a useful network of contacts – all crucial facets in a job hunt.

Andrew Scherer, Marketing Manager, Inspiring Teams and author of
Brilliant Intern

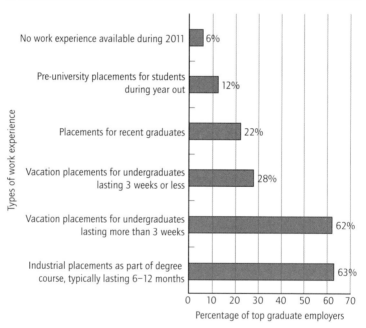

Work experience on offer from the UK's top employers in 2010–2011
Source: 'The graduate market in 2011' by High Fliers Research

Despite the vast range of opportunities presented in the table, left, with 63 per cent of employers offering some form of work experience, the market is still increasingly competitive. If students wish to undertake work experience, then they need to do their research.

How to find work experience

Having an understanding of the career you wish to explore is a great starting point for identifying work experience opportunities. Your research into your chosen career will highlight potential companies you may wish to work for. Their websites will provide information about possible work experience opportunities. Your search will be more targeted and focused if you have an idea of the company you wish to work for and the careers you wish to explore.

Careers service

The careers service at your university should be the first place you visit when trying to find an internship, placement or graduate role. As mentioned before, you are not the first student to graduate from your course, so use the experience of the careers service to establish their knowledge of recruiters, what they require, deadlines and opportunities. Careers services often have websites where positions are posted, so it is important to ensure that you are registered and receiving alerts to your email address. (Do remember to check your inbox daily and respond to emails in a timely manner.)

The websites below are also useful resources in searching for internship opportunities.

- Inspiring Interns: www.inspiringinterns.com
- Employment for Students: www.e4s.co.uk
- Prospects: www.prospects.ac.uk/work_experience.htm

- Graduate Talent Pool: http://graduatetalentpool.direct.gov. uk
- Rate My Placement: www.ratemyplacement.co.uk
- Target Jobs: http://targetjobs.co.uk

 **brilliant** tip

How can students find out about internship opportunities?

The majority of internships are advertised online. A major intern-specific portal is http://graduatetalentpool.direct.gov.uk, which is government-run and advertises placements from all over the UK. Traditional job boards are also worth checking, but are less tailored towards internships. If you have a specific sector in mind you should investigate internet forums and news sites that relate to that industry – they will often list placement vacancies. You should also consider approaching companies speculatively – often they will run schemes but not advertise them.

There are also a number of internship agencies, such as InspiringInterns.com, that specialise in matching students and graduates with opportunities. These agencies operate much like traditional recruiters, but with a sole focus on internships. Often the opportunities they advertise will be with a view to permanent hire.

One other area that has recently emerged as a job-hunting tool is social media. Hundreds of companies post vacancies – both permanent and internships – on Facebook, Twitter and LinkedIn. If you aren't already thinking of these sites as professional tools, you should start doing so.

Andrew Scherer, Marketing Manager, Inspiring Interns, and author
of *Brilliant Intern*

Your chance to shine – demonstrating your employability skills

Applying for an internship, placement or graduate role is your chance to test your product in a live environment. The feedback you gain from your application, interviews or assessment centres will help you to fine-tune your product; do you need to increase your skill set or do you have the skills, but your communication does not lend itself to marketing your features/strengths? Completing an application form and communicating your skill is an art and takes practice.

Review the skills identified in the I Brand Employability Model to see how you can best demonstrate your ability/aptitude for the role. Review all your extra-curricular activities and the tasks completed on your degree and identify the best examples to support your application: your involvement with voluntary work, sports or academic study will all provide examples to strengthen your application.

Review the employability skills developed on your degree. Complete the table overleaf, highlighting the various skills you have developed and how they relate to the skills you will need to be successful in the application process. As stated earlier, employability is built into the assessment methods, so it is important to be able to communicate how you have developed specific skills by completing your assessment.

Once you have reviewed your skills as a result of your assessment, review your development as a result of your involvement with extra-curricular activities. Highlight how your skills are relevant to the role, making specific reference to tasks or activities where you took the lead, showed initiative or negotiated a better rate.

Assessment method	Employability skills	Relevance to role

Extra-curricular activities	Skills used and developed	Relevance to role

Don't be afraid of the letter 'I'

All too often students review activities in the plural: 'we did this and we did that'. 'We' are not applying for a role so it is important to highlight the 'I' – *your* role in completing the tasks and *your* contribution. As highlighted in the I Brand Employability Model (p. xiii), your contribution will be unique. I Brand urges students to reflect on their skill set and personal traits, which ultimately defines 'What makes you stand out?' Refer back to the I Brand Employability Model – what specific skills did you use or develop as a result of completing the task? Are you a strong project manager or good team player? In relation to your I Enterprise, were you innovative in your approach and how did you persuade your team members to adopt your suggestions? Have you undertaken presentations or report-writing in the past and so were able to draw on your individual experiences to share with the group members?

Creating your I Brand is a very individual process so no brands will be the same. It is not sufficient to develop the skills. Students need to also develop their I Marketing skills to ensure that their brand is communicated effectively both in their application and in their personal appearance. Companies spend millions developing their brands and the qualities associated with them. As a new product – a graduate in the market – you need to invest the time to define the essential elements of your brand. Once you are able to define your brand, it will be easier to identify how your skills will be marketable in the graduate job market.

 **example**

Rate My Placement review

Course: BSc Computing Systems

Placement job title: Junior developer at a leading games agency

What was the application process like?

The application process consisted of three parts: sending off CV and cover letter, first interview and second interview. During the first interview we talked about general non-technical topics, while in the second one the bias was on my technical skills. During the second interview I was also given an object-orientated programming test.

What did you do on a daily basis?

My main task was developing brand-new games for two of our biggest clients. Apart from this I was also working on auto-play applications, which check the long-run payouts of our games, and producing demo versions of our products.

Highlights of the job?

The biggest highlight of the job was the release of my first game. This was a great experience and massive delight for me. I enjoyed the launch lunch, too – the food tasted great because it was earned with lots of hard work.

What was your greatest challenge?

The greatest challenge I had was to work on several projects for different departments of the company at the same time. That was great ▶

for my time-management skills, as I strived hard to meet the various deadlines.

What did you learn on your placement/internship?

In terms of technical development, I learned how to use the programming languages Flash and ActionScript, with which I had no experience before. I also practised my Java programming skills to a higher level than I had done at university.

In terms of personal development, I learned how to communicate with other members of the team in all types of situations.

What was the social life like?

The social life at Ash Gaming was truly amazing. Every month there was a poker night, sponsored by the company; every Friday we went to lunch and the pub – events that greatly strengthened the relationships between me and my colleagues – and now I feel like they are my best friends, whom I can always rely on.

Alternative routes to gaining work experience

Small and medium-sized enterprises

SMEs represent an excellent opportunity for students to gain a wide range of exposure to business processes, roles and responsibilities. The very nature of an SME's structure can provide students with opportunities to be exposed to far more responsibility than within a larger organisation. In an SME, roles are not as compartmentalised into departments, so there are more opportunities for you to excel and take on more responsibility: BUT ONLY IF YOU ARE GOOD! The recruitment process in an SME is also more informal and so reduces the number of hurdles to secure a role.

Temporary to permanent roles

Temporary roles are an excellent way to access an organisation.

Whether your role is for three or six months, you can use this time to navigate your way around the organisation to the department you want to work for. Build a network, offer your services to help, but above all else, SHINE! If you can prove your worth, then the company may be willing to take you on permanently or extend your contract. Temporary roles also help you to build experience on your CV to secure permanent positions. Unfortunately, securing temporary work is challenging as there is little training and companies expect you to 'hit the ground running'. As a result, recruitment agencies only put forward those candidates who they feel can perform the tasks required and think on their feet.

Companies and organisations usually use recruitment agencies to source temporary staff. Due to the nature of temporary roles and the fact that very little training is provided, recruiters are looking for competent candidates: candidates who can present themselves well, can think on their feet and are able to adapt to situations. How can you make your skills more attractive to recruitment consultants?

Temporary roles will usually be centred on administration duties or support functions. Your CV will need to highlight good organisational skills, computer skills, including MS Word and Excel, telephone skills and the ability to work independently.

brilliant example

I found it hard to find a graduate position when I graduated and took a temping position while I was job-hunting. The temping job was not in the field that I wanted to work in, but I was working for a company in my top ten. I offered to help members of staff with various projects and performed all of the tasks well, from filing to typing up documents and creating Excel spreadsheets. I was complimented on the standard of my work and as a result my contract was extended. I used the opportunity to network with members of staff and look for internal postings of openings within the company. Within six months I was offered a permanent junior role in an area I was interested in joining.

A business studies graduate

Job-hunting for graduate positions

Finding a graduate position will require the same level of skill as hunting for an internship. Identify the companies you wish to work for, research their deadlines for their recruitment processes and complete the applications. Finding the right company will take time, as each has its own process and set of requirements, but the more detailed your research, the more likely you are to identify the right company. When seeking graduate opportunities, company websites provide great sources of information about the range of positions available, deadlines and the career options. Other resources include sector-specific publications, the Prospects website and graduate recruitment fairs.

Companies will actively seek to recruit students through graduate recruitment fairs, both on campus and in exhibition halls. Details of these fairs will be publicised through your careers service and by searching online. Graduate fairs present a great opportunity to speak with the employer and glean any additional information about the company and what companies are looking for in graduates.

 **brilliant** dos and don'ts

The dos and don'ts of job-hunting

Do

✔ **Think of a handful of companies that you really admire/ want to work for and research them** – What graduate opportunities do they have? What's the culture like? What does the company stand for? What is the future for this company? How can you apply? What is their recruitment process?

Don't

✘ **Make hundreds of applications half-heartedly** – It's really easy to spot an application that has been made to hundreds of companies generically (you even see the odd copy and paste job!) and it really doesn't make a good impression. If you can't be bothered to make the application, then why would a potential employer bother to read it?

Beckie Fish, Graduate Recruitment Advisor, Sainsbury's plc

Plan B

Due to the increasingly competitive nature of the graduate market, it is important to have a back-up plan if you are unable to secure a position on a graduate scheme. Other options to consider would be temporary positions, as outlined above, or full-time permanent roles. There are many ways to navigate your career and today it is important to exhaust as many options as possible. Companies will recruit graduates into permanent roles within the company. Use recruitment websites and career-specific websites to research opportunities. Your careers service may also be able to help you.

 **brilliant** recap

- Graduates with no work experience will struggle to secure a place on a graduate scheme.
- Of the top graduate employers, 63 per cent offer some form of work experience.
- There are three main types of work experience: job shadowing, internships and placements.
- Small and medium-sized enterprises provide a range of opportunities for students to gain exposure to business processes, roles and responsibilities.
- Do not ignore the value of a temporary role – it can lead to a permanent position.
- Be focused in your search for a graduate position – target specific companies you want to work for.
- Have a back-up plan if you are unable to secure a graduate role.

CHAPTER 5

Developing a Brilliant you

Developing employability skills is a never ending journey with lots of twists and turns, and continual opportunities to explore and discover

n this chapter we will review the elements of the I Brand Employability Model and how you can use it to develop your individual brand to increase your employability. Other factors in your development will also be considered, including developing an elevator pitch, mentoring and networking. Each of these elements will add value to your portfolio of skills and increase your chance of success.

For reference the I Brand Employability Model is reproduced overleaf.

The model consists of three levels.

1 The degree.

2 Generic employability skills, including:

- leadership
- team-working
- positive attitude
- communication
- problem-solving
- commercial awareness
- numeracy
- computer literacy
- cultural sensitivity.

3 Your individual contribution, which is denoted by:

- I Experience
- I Network
- I Enterprise
- I Marketing.

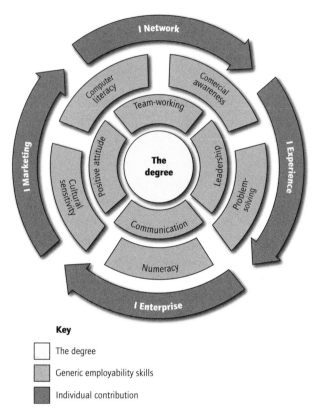

Key

☐ The degree

▨ Generic employability skills

▨ Individual contribution

The I Brand Employability Model

Your degree

There is no doubt that your degree is at the heart of your experience at university, but you also need to recognise the additional layers within the model. Your degree undeniably provides you with a technical and generic skill set, which makes you proficient within your field of study, but extra-curricular activities can broaden your experience and portfolio of skills. A degree allows you to enter the arena, but it is your involvement in developing relevant employability skills that will differentiate you from the competition and help you secure a graduate position.

Generic employability skills

The core generic skills outlined in the model gives students an indication of graduate recruiters' expectations. These skills are generic in nature and are not industry-specific. They form the basis of standard requirements expected from graduates. As a result, regardless of your discipline, you must be able to provide a practical demonstration of how you have developed these skills throughout your work experience and extra-curricular activities. By actively engaging with the development of these skills you will be able to provide comprehensive examples to support your applications and during the interview processes for all graduate positions.

Use the list of skills below to rate yourself against.

Generic employability skills	Definition	Score
Leadership	Self-starter, organisational skills, influencing and motivational skills	
Team-working	Ability to work with others, listen, contribute, negotiate	
Commercial awareness	Understanding key factors that impact business performance and customer satisfaction	
Problem-solving	Provide innovative solutions and recommendations	
Communication	Use oral and written communication effectively	
Numeracy	A general understanding of figures and an ability to manipulate data	
Computer literacy	Basic IT skills and competence in standard IT packages, e.g. Microsoft Office	
Positive attitude	A willingness and drive to try new ideas	

Which of the skills are your strengths and weaknesses? Grade yourself on a scale of 1–5 in relation to the skills listed. Now use your scores to develop an action plan with SMART goals to identify how, while at university, you are going to develop these skills. Complete the table below for each skill.

Goal
Specific
Measurable
Achievable
Realistic
Timely

Individual contribution

The individual elements of the model recognise students' individuality. Every student will have a different history and experiences that will separate them, so we cannot ignore students' backgrounds and how this impacts, both positively and negatively, on their future development. Students will also interact with the different elements of the model based on their own personal preferences and personalities and, as a result, no two students can have the same experience.

I Experience

Your individual experiences will impact on how you develop your employability skills. You may be a mature student returning to university to retrain or the first in your family to attend university or, perhaps, a single parent. Regardless, you cannot ignore your personal story. Your goals, ambition and drive will dictate to what extent these skills are ingrained into your profile.

l Network

Networking is an essential ingredient when developing employability skills. Your ability to network will help you identify possible job opportunities. How you manage your network, build your network and utilise your network is a very personal activity. The results of networking will vary for every individual, as the success of networking is dependent upon your ability to develop a rapport and create a memorable impression. Your network is also based upon who you know and their wider network. Some students have the benefit of being able to tap into their parents' network or that of friends of friends. As a result, the extent of your network is also dependent upon your individual connections.

l Enterprise

Entrepreneurial spirit is within you. It is part of your DNA. The ability to find solutions or make recommendations that project a company or product beyond its current constraints is an inbuilt talent. Entrepreneurial spirit is an individual characteristic and so it is important to recognise that despite the opportunities to develop employability skills, students may or may not be entrepreneurial in their approach.

l Marketing

Ultimately, it is how you present yourself to potential employers, both through written and verbal communication, that will determine your ability to secure a position. This ranges from your choice of words to the way you dress to even the way you walk. All of theses choices will reflect your individual preference and hence cannot be replicated by another candidate. As a result it is important to recognise that, despite having the same employability skills, these will be adopted in different ways and conveyed using different experiences to reflect your individuality.

I Brand

The circular nature of the model indicates the continuous process. Developing your employability skills is continuous. With the advancement of technology, the changing landscape and development of economies has a significant impact on your skills. You can't afford to stand still. Once you secure a position, your next goal is to keep the position. Updating your skills is an essential part of the current employment climate. Those who let their skills lapse often face redundancy or the need to retrain as their skills become out of date. As a result you are also continually updating your network, looking for new enterprising ways to conduct business, learning from your experiences and continually updating your brand.

brilliant tip

Q What advice would you give students to increase their employability while at university?

A **Get a part-time job** – it can really help if you have some sort of work experience, whether that's a customer service role in retail or as waiter/ waitress in a restaurant. This will show potential employers that you have some experiences/skills in customer service, working to deadlines, communications and team-working, etc. – all of which is essential in any career.

A **Use your careers service** – careers advisors are really helpful and have a good idea of what careers are available to you. A good careers advisor will have strong links with companies that may be beneficial for you.

A **Go to skills sessions run by your university** – skills sessions are usually run by volunteers from all sorts of companies that work with the university so will be able to provide you with useful skills/knowledge and will help you build relationships with prospective employers.

▶

A **Go to the careers fairs run by your university** – this is a great way of finding out from the 'horse's mouth' about what opportunities companies have for graduates. Do go prepared, though! Find out who is going to be there and what you would like to find out from them – the people at the stand could be the recruitment team, so make the right impression.

A **Try to get an internship while studying** – some degrees require you to do a year in industry, which is a good way to get some work experience and looks great on your CV. Lots of companies also offer internships over the summer and again this is a really good opportunity to get some work experience and discover if the company's right for you. Another great benefit is that some companies use internships as a pipeline to fill their graduate schemes or other positions, so it could lead to a permanent role.

Beckie Fish, Graduate Recruitment Advisor, Sainsbury's plc

Elevator pitch

An elevator pitch is a concise way of stating who you are and what you do, but including an interesting fact about yourself. The reason it is called an elevator pitch is that it denotes the time you have to make an impression between the ground floor and the top floor on an elevator ride. You should be able to introduce yourself within one minute and convey an interesting fact about your skills. Make sure you know your speciality; what makes you unique.

brilliant timesaver

Imagine you get in the lift with an individual you admire. How would you introduce yourself to create an impression? Practise developing a concise introduction stating who you are, what you do and a unique fact about how you perform your job!

Mentors

A mentor is a valuable asset at any point in your career. Mentors can provide an insight to possible career options, advice prior to an interview and a sounding board for all major decisions. Mentoring can be part of an established programme or an informal relationship. To make the most of a mentoring relationship, take the time to identify what you hope to gain from the relationship, establish clear goals and aims at the start and schedule all of your meetings for the duration of the programme. Having an experienced mentor can be a benefit both during and after the programme. If you really connect, your mentor relationship can extend past the mentoring scheme to become part of your personal network.

Building your network

 Six degrees of separation

'I am bound to everyone on this planet by a trail of six people'
Frigyes Karinthy, 1929

A broad network of people will help you to gain an insight into a world of opportunity. Friends of friends will be able to provide you with access to people, information and opportunities. Your network will consist of individuals who are like-minded, but also individuals who would not immediately be seen as your peer. The broader your network, the wider your reach.

Traditional face-to-face networking can involve formal networking events, but also casual conversations over the photocopier. Try not to always see networking as what's in it for you, but look at the wider picture. How can you create situations that will benefit others? Ultimately people will remember you when an opportunity arises that is of interest to you.

With the increase of social networking it is just as important to build an online network. LinkedIn provides a platform for social networking with professionals, giving rise to opportunities to connect with alumni, industry professionals and business-related groups. The first step in networking online is to create a LinkedIn profile.

brilliant tip

Five tips for creating a winning profile on LinkedIn

1 Enter your full name and add a professional photo.

2 Provide details about your current status, in as much detail as possible, so that the relevance of your experience can be matched against possible job vacancies.

3 Previous work experience – state where you have worked or any voluntary positions held.

4 Place of study – list your university as this will help identify former students and any alumni groups.

5 Contact settings states how other LinkedIn users can contact you. There is a range of options from job opportunities to requests to reconnect.

Your profile is key to networking online as this is how others will find you. LinkedIn can also make it easier for you to not only research companies but also find out about new vacancies. LinkedIn provides you with an overview of the company and possible opportunities. If anyone in your network works or is connected to the company, LinkedIn will highlight how you can be recommended through your personal network. This is an excellent mechanism for utilising your network. The discussion groups facilitate discussions with professionals in your chosen career, as well as give you the ability to find out more about career choices.

Other professional networking sites include Plaxo (www.plaxo.com) and Ecademy (www.ecademy.com).

 example

Be proactive with the faculty

It's easy to get lost in the crowd at university when 'classes' can often be lectures addressed to hundreds of students. To stand out, take a proactive role in getting to know your lecturers, especially your advisors. Your professors can be invaluable sources of advice, guidance and networking support in the 'real world' since many of them work or have relationships in the business world as well as the campus community.

Big brother – networking sites

Remember your profile information is now out there ... potentially for everyone to peruse. Prospective employers/networkers/colleagues now have access to pictures of you ... Keep it appropriate if you are going to use your profile for professional networking.

Attend a conference

Upon joining a professional organisation, consider attending a conference or event sponsored by the group. There you will meet professionals already working in the field who are more than willing to assist the next generation. You may also receive publications from the organisation that list job openings and career advice for young professionals interested in the field.

Get carded

Consider creating a 'networking card'. This is simply a business card for people who are not yet in business. A simple card with your name and email address or phone number is all you need.

Collecting business cards

When preparing for your future or developing a professional network, business cards are like golden tickets. Collect business cards when meeting people and always make sure to follow up with an email or letter soon after. Keep the business cards you collect in a safe place for quick and easy reference later on.

Adopt a mentor … or two or three

This is especially important at university, when you're at a critical point in your career development. If you can align yourself with people already practising in your selected field, you can learn all kinds of insights that you won't learn in the classroom. When you let it be known that you're looking for someone to help guide you in your career, you may be surprised at how many people offer to lend a hand.

Carol Rene, *The Students' Guide to Networking*

brilliant example

I graduated with a third-class degree, but I still secured a graduate position upon graduation. It was my extra-curricular activities that impressed my interviewers. I was able to demonstrate practical examples of employability skills and my achievements. I had run several successful events at university, helped run the SU radio, raised £1000 for charity. What I lacked in a degree, I made up for with my extra-curricular activities. Sure, I wish I had graduated with a first, but I am now studying for my Masters!

A human resources management graduate

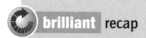 recap

- The I Brand Employability Model defines three layers to developing your employability:

  - the degree

  - generic employability skills

  - individual contribution.

- Employability is a continuous cycle, as you need to continually update your skills.

- Develop an action plan to identify the skills you need to develop.

- Find a mentor to help navigate both your degree and your career!

- Networking is an excellent way to increase your opportunities – you never know who the people you meet can introduce you to!

- Create a LinkedIn profile – it is important to have an online profile to support your personal networking efforts.

CHAPTER 6

Communicating
your Brilliance

Even when you are silent you are still
communicating

lways remember, communication is not just verbal, it's about how you present yourself, the accuracy of your written word, your body language and your attitude. All of your actions communicate a trait of your professionalism. A badly spelt application speaks volumes about future communications with the company's clients. If you are unable to present yourself in a professional manner, how will you represent the company? This chapter focuses on opportunities for you to communicate your professionalism in a manner sought after by graduate employers.

CVs, covering letters and application forms

The majority of companies have moved away from receiving curriculum vitaes (CVs) in favour of their own application forms. This is primarily to encourage candidates to complete a specific application in response to the company's requirements. However, this does not always work, as candidates still copy and paste responses from one application to another, sometimes without even changing the company's name. Oops! Companies often find the standard of applications received is better with the use of their own application form. Previously students would not think about the specific role requirements and would send the same CV to several companies in the hope that one would invite them for an interview. The application form in most cases forces students to match their strengths to the requirements of the role they are applying for.

The CV is still an acceptable form of applying for some roles, but also serves as a very useful marketing tool for undergraduates. The CV encourages students to evaluate their skills in relation to their specific discipline, extra-curricular activities and current part-time work and analyse what skills they have developed. Often students feel they have very little to offer, but if you complete the following exercise you will find that throughout your time at university you will have developed a range of skills.

Role	Action	Skills developed
Examples: Saturday sales assistant for three years	Team leader for three members of staff. Organised team shifts, responsible for organising section stock-take and handling customer queries	Commitment Customer service Organisational skills Managerial skills Project management Punctuality

Complete the table and see what skills you have developed. Use this information to build your CV.

 **example**

It was only when I sat with the careers adviser that I realised I had developed valuable employability skills. I did not see the value in my part-time job or the voluntary work I had been doing for an hour every week for the last two years. This exercise was a real confidence boost, as I had not seen myself in this light before. I had a really clear idea of what I could offer to an employer.

An English graduate

Formatting your CV

A standard CV will be two pages in length and contain the following:

● personal details

- contact details
- qualifications
- personal statement
- work experience
- voluntary and extra-curricular activities (optional)
- hobbies and interests.

 **example**

Good CV checklist

Name

Home and term-time address

Email

Telephone (both mobile and landline)

Personal statement

Qualifications listed in chronological order (most recent first)

Institutions listed

Dates attended

Relevant subjects

Dissertation topic

Work experience with summary of duties

Summary of relevant skills and levels attained

Summary of interests

 **brilliant** example

The figure below shows how *not* to write your CV!

Curriculum vitae G I Sajob Address Email darknight@hotmail.com 21 Secret Road Tel: 020 8123 4567 London E10 4SU Mob: 07927 112233	Give your full name. Ensure your contact details are accurate and avoid the use of an unprofessional email address. Record a professional answering message on both numbers
Personal statement I have worked as a sales assistant for a year and volunteer on Thursdays at the local girlguides	Your personal statement should be a WOW statement about you; a reason why employers would consider buying your product! Show how your skills are relevant to the role you are applying for. Review the format and fonts used to ensure consistency
Qualifications GCSE English Lang: B English Lit: A Maths: A* RE: C Science: B PE: B Business Studies: C IT: B A2 Level Economics: B Business studies: A AS Level	When listing qualifications, use chronological order with the most recent at the top. Clearly state dates of attendance and the name of the institution. Give details of the main topics covered in your degree, especially those relevant to the role

English: A Economics: B Business Studies: A **Degree:** Economics and Business: 2:1	
Work experience Topshop Saturday Sale Assistant B & Q Store Assistant	Clearly state dates of employment. Give an overview of your role, highlighting relevant skills: 'Assisted customers, providing speed and accuracy on the checkout to ensure management of queues and customer satisfaction.' OR 'First line of contact for customers with queries on the shop floor. Resolved customer queries to ensure a good shopping experience'
Interests Travelling, social networking and reading	How do these interests add value to your application? Try to highlight interests that demonstrate your ability to interact, communicate and/or help others. This area of the application is weak and the student needs to engage in additional extra-curricular activity to strengthen the application
Skills Strong communication and interpersonal skill Computer literate	Highlight skills that are transferable to the world of work. Avoid spelling mistakes as accuracy is essential. Show which computer skills you have acquired
References available on request	

Contact details

Email address
Avoid using unprofessional email addresses. Either opt to use your university email address or create an online email address that simply uses your name. Do not use the fun email addresses that you use with your friends: foxylady@hotmail.com, prince@gmail.com or darkknight@hotmail.com. These email addresses communicate the wrong message to an employer. Always ensure that you check your email on a daily basis, as tardy responses reflect the timeliness of your responses to future clients.

Language
Text language has become an acceptable means of talking among your friends, but remember that applying for jobs requires a more formal response and it is not acceptable for text-speak to transfer into this arena.

Voicemail message
When applying for roles, remove any joke voicemails and record a standard message asking the caller to leave their name and contact number. The use of music, jokes or funny phrases should be avoided.

Answering your phone
When answering your phone, be professional; you never know what opportunity lies the other end of the line. A badly answered call indicates to a potential employer that you lack customer service skills. Is this how you will answer the phone to their clients?

Qualifications
List your qualifications in chronological order, stating the institution from which you gained the qualification, the date and the grade. Qualifications should be listed with the most recent first. Ensure accuracy in this section as employers will want to see certificates supporting all of your qualifications.

brilliant tip

Pre-employment screening is utilised by companies to verify the information provided by a candidate when applying for, or being offered, a new job. This ensures there has been complete honesty and full disclosure from the candidates at an early stage of the recruitment process, which substantially reduces the risk of a company investing time and financial resources in an inappropriate hire.

When applying for graduate roles, candidates should:

● provide correct identification details, which can be supported with a valid passport or driving licence

● ensure all qualifications can be verified by the institution from which they were attained

● declare any criminal offences, where relevant to the role

● ensure all previous employment information and references are accurate and true.

There is a wide range of checks available, from previous employment reference checks, credit checks and criminal record checks, right the way through to international referencing, educational qualification checks, directorship searches and identity verification. These checks can be applied on a selected basis, depending on the requirements of the hiring company, type of position the candidate is applying for and the level of risk that the candidate will have in his or her new role.

With more and more businesses realising the importance of background screening and, crucially, the potential impact of not screening a new candidate effectively, it is almost certain that candidates will experience some form of pre-employment screening.

Rupert Emson, Vero Screening

Personal statement

The personal statement is a summary of your brilliance. In this section, highlight your achievements, strengths and key skills. Remember to review the skills required for the role you are applying for and ensure you make reference to these skills here. An employer should read this statement and think WOW! This is where I would encourage you to blow your own trumpet!

Work experience

As an undergraduate your work experience may be limited, but list all of your previous employment, starting with the most recent. For each post state:

● job title

● date of employment (including start date and end date)

● brief description of the role, highlighting key achievements: employee of the month awards, cost-saving recommendations, commitment, customer service skills, etc.

If, on the other hand, your work experience is quite extensive, include the last ten years with a summary of anything of significance before this. If there are any gaps in your dates, provide a note explaining the reason for this, i.e. July 2007–September 2008: gap year – travelling around the world.

Voluntary and extra-curricular activities

Only include this section if you have been active in these areas. Often if students lack in work experience, they can demonstrate their employability skills through their extra-curricular activities. Highlight the skills relevant to the role to emphasise your suitability.

Hobbies and interests

Include a few lines about your hobbies and interests; they can make an interesting talking point.

brilliant dos and don'ts

Do

✔ Be meticulous – spelling mistakes, inconsistency in dates and general errors instantly land your CV in the reject pile.

✔ Spend the time making your CV as marketable as possible – writing a CV is not a quick task.

Don't

✘ Use the same CV for several jobs – employers want to see how you will fit a specific role, so amend your CV to the skills required for each application.

✘ Use cheap paper – the quality and cleanliness of the paper reflect you as a person!

Covering letters

A covering letter is a brief letter that tells the reader:

● why you are writing to them

● why they should read your CV or application

● thank them for their time.

Format of a covering letter

A covering letter should have three main paragraphs, which highlight the role you are applying for, why you are interested in the role and how your strengths demonstrate the competencies outlined in the job description. The standard of your covering letter sets the tone of your application – incorrect spellings, how it is addressed and the wording all make statements about your attention to detail and the level of effort applied to constructing the letter. All too often companies receive letters addressed to the wrong person, with silly spelling mistakes and not specifically tailored to the role being applied for. Remember, this is your marketing document and the presentation and content will be the deciding factor as to whether or not a company will take your application further.

What makes a good covering letter?

The basics

- Use plain white photocopy paper (expensive paper is not essential; the selling point will be the format and the content).

- Length – one A4 page.

- Address the letter correctly – if the name is stated, use 'Dear Miss Smith', ending the letter with 'Yours sincerely'. If the name is unstated, use 'Dear sir or madam' ending the letter with 'Yours faithfully'. Where possible, do try to find out who the letter should be addressed to as it makes it easier if you wish to follow up.

- Quote the reference for the job (if there is one stated).

First paragraph

The first paragraph should provide a strong introduction and reason for your letter. Make reference to the role you are applying for and where you found the advert. Highlight why you are interested in the role and also the company.

Second paragraph

Review the job description and demonstrate how your skills relate to the competencies listed in the job description. Be very clear and concise as to how your skills match those required by the company. Summarise your overall strengths and the reasons you would be an asset to the company.

Third paragraph

In the final paragraph, state any particular dates that you will be unavailable for interview. Do thank the employer for the time spent reading your covering letter.

End

Yours sincerely/yours faithfully depending on who the letter is addressed to (see under 'The basics', left), followed by your signature and your name printed in full underneath.

Common errors with covering letters

- A generic letter, not customised to reflect the skills and competencies highlighted in the job description.
- Addressed to the wrong person.
- Silly spelling mistakes, which would have been spotted with the use of spellcheck and proofreading.
- The letter does not stress the reasons for the candidate being the best person for the job.
- Too long – covering letters should be clear and concise.
- A scattergun approach, sending letters with no specific relation to role or company.

Application forms

Whether or not you are invited for an interview will be based on how well you complete the application form. The form represents your first formal communication with the company, so it is important to give a good first impression. When completing online or written applications, be clear as to when the form needs to be submitted; applications received after the deadline are not even considered!

Read through the job selection criteria and the job description and map these against your skills and experience. This will enable you to clearly demonstrate your suitability. Use a wide variety of examples, both academic and non-academic. Read and answer all of the questions! An incomplete form will be rejected.

Quotes from graduate applications received by Gary Argent, Business Operations Manager at the Association of Graduate Recruiters during his ten years of reading graduate applications:

Question: Please tell us about your greatest achievement.

Answer: 'Sleeping.'

Question: Give an example of a time when you provided a high level of customer service.

Answer: 'Further details available on request.'

Question: Please describe the factors that make you want to work for X.

Answer: 'Money. Power. Sex.'

Question: Tell us what you learned from your work experience.

Answer: 'Job: checkout operator at X. This job taught me to value the end of the day.'

Question: Please tell us if you have any objections to defence work.

Answer 1: 'I'm a lover, not a fighter.'

Answer 2: 'Not allowed – I wear spectacles.'

If you are completing a handwritten application, photocopy it first. Do several drafts before attempting to complete the actual form. Remember there is no excuse for mistakes and misspelt words on your application. With online applications, you are usually able to save the form or your progress to date. Ensure that you draft your answer and read it through before submitting. Use your careers service and book a skills session on CVs and applications.

brilliant tip

Read the questions and answer them; don't just answer what you think they are asking, really read it through. Use the STAR technique to structure answers: S – Situation, T – Task, A – Action, R – Result. This will ensure your answer reads well and you include all relevant facts. Make sure you don't just copy and paste from another application and people do read through every application so just putting key words down and thinking a computer is going to pick them up doesn't work! Use as many interesting examples as possible, but don't lie! Always check your grammar and spelling and get someone else to read it over before you submit it.

Claire Thomas, Graduate Marketing Manager, Centrica

Pre-interview

Dress code

To dress up or to dress down? Many organisations have adopted a dress-down policy in relation to staff who are not customer-facing. As a result, on a day-to-day basis staff can be seen to be wearing very casual wear to work. Always remember they are on the inside of the organisation and already work there. You, on the other hand, are trying to get on the other side of the wall. As a result it is always best to create a good first impression by adopting a more traditional sense of dress for an interview. This way the company knows that if you are required to present to a client you can dress appropriately.

brilliant example

I was so embarrassed when I turned up for my interview 'creatively dressed' and all the other candidates were in suits. It really knocked my confidence. I performed terribly in the interview as I just could not stop thinking about ▶

how under-dressed I was and how they must wonder if I even owned a suit. Needless to say, I was not appointed to the role. Always dress up, as employers know how you will present yourself to potential clients.

A digital art graduate

What do we mean by a 'traditional sense of dress'? A navy blue or black suit. This is applicable to both males and females. Women should avoid tops that reveal too much cleavage, heels over two inches and tight-fitting clothing. A court shoe with up to a two-inch heel would be more suitable. Avoid making any fashion statements, so piercings, radical hairstyles and tattoos should be avoided at all costs. These may be appropriate while at university, but do not transfer well into the world of work. If you have dyed your hair a bright colour while studying, dye it back before applying for jobs! Once you get the job you can be as radical as you like, when you have proven your worth, but until then stay within the guidelines.

Males	Females
Navy blue or black suit	Navy blue or black suit (knee-length skirt)
White shirt (ironed)	White blouse (ironed)
Plain tie	Simple jewellery and make-up
Polished black shoes	Polished court shoes (up to a two-inch heel)
Black briefcase	Black briefcase

If you are confident in the way you are dressed this will translate into your overall appearance of being a confident candidate. Dress to impress as first impressions are formed within the first 30 seconds.

Planning your journey

Arriving late speaks volumes to interviewers. In just ten minutes you have demonstrated:

● an inability to project-manage your journey

● a lack of organisational skills

● a lack of time management

● lack of respect for their time.

As you can imagine, unless there has been a natural disaster there is no excuse for being late. Ways to avoid being late include:

● a practice run of the journey, so on the day you know exactly where you are going and how to get there

● plan your journey so you arrive at least 30 minutes early and allow time for train delays or cancellations

● if the journey involves you travelling long distances, perhaps see if you can stay with a friend or relative who lives closer.

Researching the company

Knowing about the company and the industry is an important part of interview preparation. This demonstrates to the interviewer that you not only want the job but also want to work for their company. Having an understanding of the industry, their competitors and the challenges the company faces show initiative on your part and will make your answers more relevant.

There are many sources to access information about companies:

● company website

● annual report

● industry magazines

● Google alerts for current information.

The handshake

A crushing handshake can leave the interviewer dreading

shaking your hand on exit, but a weak, wet handshake is not impressive either. It is therefore important to practise shaking hands to ensure you have a firm handshake, which exudes confidence.

Five key steps to a Brilliant handshake:

1   make eye contact and smile

2   extend your hand

3   take a firm grip

4   shake the hand up and down two or three times

5   say your name.

Getting this right takes practice, so use your careers service, your friends or lecturers to not only practise but also receive feedback on your handshake. It is important that you get this right as this brief exchange makes a statement about your confidence and self-esteem.

Preparing a presentation

Communication skills are an essential part of any role and students may be asked to prepare a short presentation as part of the interview process. As with any presentation, it is essential that you understand the task. The key to a successful presentation is as follows:

● adopt a clear structure

● use bullet points and avoid lengthy paragraphs

● use approximately one slide for each minute of the presentation, i.e. a ten-minute presentation equals ten slides

● practise, practise and practise!

brilliant tip

As I sat in the waiting area I knew I had prepared the perfect presentation. It may have taken days, but I was confident it was what they were looking for. This could be it, my final interview! I tapped my pocket for the hundredth time to ensure that my USB was still in my pocket. My name was called and I walked confidently into the room. I was given five minutes to set up; I was nervous and confident all at the same time. As I inserted my USB and tried to open my file, a warning sign came up stating my file was not compatible. I clicked to reopen the file and the same message came up. The interviewer must have seen the distress on my face. 'Is there anything wrong?' she asked. My confidence ebbed away along with my presentation, which I had saved in the latest version of the software. and their computers were not just one but two versions behind. Needless to say, my presentation did not go to plan and it definitely was not my final interview, but I learnt the hard way: do not always save your presentation in the latest software format and always have a printout handy. Due to cost, companies do not always upgrade immediately to the newest version of software.

A business information technology graduate

Preparing questions

Don't forget that the interview is your chance to find out more about the organisation, so come prepared with a few questions about it. Your research of the company may have raised some questions, but try to avoid questions about salary. Although this may be at the forefront of your mind, with your increasing student loans, avoid focusing purely on the financial aspect of the role. The job advert should have given some indication of salary bracket.

Questions can focus on the following areas.

● What are the next steps following this interview?
● What is the career development and progression for someone at this level in your organisation?
● Use your research to formulate a question in relation to the company's current climate.

brilliant dos and don'ts

Do

✔ Research the company and set up a 'Google alert' with the company's name a couple of weeks before the interview – you will be sent links to all news articles relating to them, so at interview you will have some fresh material to talk about.

✔ Think about why you want to join that particular company/ industry. They want to see your enthusiasm specifically for them; anyone can say generic things about why they want a job.

Don't

✘ Forget to prepare how you are getting to the interview, what you are wearing, the name of the person you are going to see, any extra material you need, such as CV, ID, calculator, dissertation. Being prepared and arriving well in advance will ensure you are calm before the interview.

Claire Thomas, Graduate Marketing Manager, Centrica

Do

✔ Prepare, research and understand the company you are applying to – they will want to understand your motivation for applying.

✔ Think about the activities/work placements/projects that you have been involved in and consider how you could use them to demonstrate key business competencies, such as leadership,

▶

influencing, team-work, etc. Organisations will all use slightly
different words but the key competencies they are looking for
will be similar.

Don't

✗ Try to over-rehearse because you may be thrown by different
interview styles or techniques.

Helen Alkin, Recruitment Manager, Marks and Spencer plc

Interview skills – putting your best foot forward

The interview is your chance to demonstrate why you are more
suitable for this job than any other candidate. Central to a successful interview is preparation, but how do you prepare for the
unknown? This section aims to provide information about the
format of the interview, the structure and possible questions.
More importantly, the tools for you to communicate your excellence without saying a word!

The format of the interview

Interviews vary depending upon the size of the company and
the sector. Often the invitation to interview will provide more
information. Types of interview are discussed below.

A panel interview

Representatives for the panel will be drawn from interested
parties in the role they are recruiting for: human resources, the
manager, technical specialist (if applicable). The panel will sit
in a row on one side of the table with you on the other; yes, the
same format as a firing squad! A panel interview is not as bad
as it sounds. Prior to attending you will be given the names of
the panellists. Shake hands with each member of the panel and,
when answering their questions, try to make eye contact.

A series of interviews

Most interviews will adopt the format of a first and second interview followed by an assessment centre or series of tests. The interviews will usually be conducted by the line manager, followed by a senior manager accompanied by a representative from human resources. In some cases, the interview with human resources is conducted separately. The benefit of having one-to-one interviews is that you can build a rapport on an individual basis.

A telephone interview

Telephone interviews are becoming more frequent. Candidates will be given a time to expect a call from the interviewer. The details of the name and person will be provided before the interview. Be ready! Don't be caught on the hop. Find a quiet place to take the call. How you perform will determine if you are selected for the next round of interviews.

 **timesaver**

When attending an interview I always bring along the interview letter, just in case I forget the contact name due to nerves. The letter also reminds me of any specific details of where to go on arrival.

A business graduate

Interview structure

Whether a panel interview or a one-to-one, the structure of the interview will be similar. The interviewers will try to relax you with a general question, i.e. on your journey or a question about the weather. Do not ramble on and on about this unless you are going for an interview with London Transport. Recognise that this is just a warm-up question, so keep it brief. The interviewer will then ask you a series of questions that draw on the selection criteria and the skills required for the post. Tailor your responses and examples to the question being asked. Take a few minutes to ensure you understand the question and have a good example to support your answer.

Interview questions

What will they ask you? The job selection criteria and the job description will provide you with the hints and tips you need to prepare for possible interview questions. A good framework to use is STAR: Situation, Task, Action, Result. This framework encourages you to provide specific examples to demonstrate both the competencies and the behavioural criteria outlined in the selection criteria. Read both the job description and selection criteria and identify key skills (usually marked as E for essential).

Situation – Think of a situation when you have demonstrated the skill. Try to use examples that are drawn from your course, but also from your extra-curricular activities.

Task – What was your aim/purpose?

Action – What was your role? Outline your actions.

Result – What was the outcome?

Give examples of when you have demonstrated the skills listed below	Situation	Task	Action	Result
Leadership skills				
Team-work skills				
Organisational skills				
Project management				
Initiative				
Commitment				
Determination				

Here are some other possible questions.

Why do you want to work for ...?

What do you think you can offer ...?

What are your strengths and weaknesses?

brilliant dos and don'ts

Do

✔ Listen to the questions or brief you are being given to ensure that you don't go off track.

✔ Dress appropriately, in line with the role that you have applied for.

✔ Give yourself time to read, understand and plan for the exercise and think about the points you want to make – for assessment centres specifically.

Don't

✗ Worry if you need to take a few seconds to formulate your answer in your head before responding.

✗ Panic at an assessment centre, even if you feel one exercise has gone badly – the decision will be based on your performance and each competency will be rated more than once, so all is not lost.

Helen Alkin, Recruitment Manager, Marks and Spencer plc

Do

✔ Sell yourself; don't say things like, 'We did this ...' say, 'I did this ...'. You have done very well to get the interview, so make the most of the time by talking about all the things you have achieved and give examples of how you did this, how you meet the company's objectives and employee ethos.

✔ Use as many examples in your answers as possible. This will show off your range of experience and make your interviewer interested in what you are saying. Using the same examples is

▶

boring and doesn't make the most of what you have done. Use a range of academic and non-academic answers.

Don't

✗ Panic if they ask you a 'curve ball' question – always take a few moments to think about your answer. Even if it is something you know how to answer, it shows to the interviewer you have thought about what you are going to say. If you jump straight in, you may get lost halfway through; that could make you panic and also make you look unprepared. If you do lose your way, keep calm and take another moment to think before you speak again.

Claire Thomas, Graduate Marketing Manager, Centrica

Non-verbal communication – communicating your excellence without saying a word

During the interview it's not always what you *say* that makes a difference, it can be what you *do*! As stated earlier in the chapter, your appearance makes an impact on how you are perceived. Other factors to consider are your posture, facial expression and your walk. These actions all talk to the employer about your suitability, so make sure they are sending the right message. If you are prone to slouching when you walk or sit, make sure you correct this for the interview. A confident walk sends the right message when you enter the room.

Eye contact is essential; try to build rapport with the interviewer by looking at them when you speak. If you are addressing a panel interview, make eye contact with the person who is asking the questions, but during your response try to look at the other members of the panel as well. This is easier said than done: it takes practice. Make use of your careers service to practise your interview techniques.

 tip

Your exit is just as important as your entrance. I was so excited that the interview had gone well. I was able to answer all the questions. My preparation had paid off. We shook hands and I turned to exit. Forgetting that we were in a glass office, I walked straight into the glass door. I tried to recover quickly, but you could see the amazement on their faces. I composed myself and exited successfully on my second attempt. My advice – stay focused till the end of the interview, your exit needs to be clean. By the way, I did get the job in the end!

An IT graduate

Psychometric tests

Psychometric tests are often included in the selection process and can take various forms. The most common tests include:

- verbal reasoning
- numerical reasoning
- personality.

Companies will often inform you prior to your interview which of the above will be involved in the test.

How do you prepare? Prior to attending you can take practice tests. Your careers service will often have a selection of practice tests, but you can also go online to www.shl.com, who create the majority of the tests used by employers, and practise sample tests online.

Assessment centres

Companies often save the best till last, so the assessment centres are often the final hurdle in the interview process. Due to the expense of running an assessment centre, only the candidates who have true potential are invited. What can you expect? Assessment centres allow companies to observe you in a range of settings to see how you cope. As a result, the assessment centre is made up of a series of individual and group tasks. An observer will be assigned to each candidate and make notes and grade you in relation to the selection criteria. Often you are not required to prepare any material, as the observer wishes to observe how you approach the given tasks and your interactions with the rest of the group. There are no right or wrong answers to many of the exercises, but they are interested in your methods of deduction and handling of data. The exercises can include those listed in the table overleaf.

These exercises enable the company to observe a number of skills, which you will have discussed in previous interviews. The assessment centre allows them to observe first-hand how you meet their selection criteria. Skills tested can include:

- communication
- team-working
- decision-making
- initiative
- leadership.

Post-interview

The interview is over, there is nothing you can do to change your performance, but it is good to reflect upon what went well and what you would change for next time. Practise learning from every interview, as the more interviews you do the more expe-rienced and ready you will be for the next one. Reflect on the examples you used to answer the questions. Were they sufficient? Were you clear in explaining your role and the actions you took? Don't be impatient and call the company the next day for the result; wait to be contacted.

Task	Description	Tips
Mini case-study	The mini case-study will provide the information for a given task. Candidates will be required to use the information to formulate a response	Don't panic! Build your response. Identify factors that will affect the decision; highlight additional information needed; state the reasoning for your response
Presentation or report	The presentation or report is often linked to the mini case-study and candidates are asked to present their results either verbally or in a report	Present a structured response! Practise your presentation skills beforehand. The careers service will have skills sessions available
In-tray exercise	This exercise is as it sounds. Candidates are given an in-tray consisting of emails, memos, messages, etc. and the task involves prioritising and preparing responses to the requests	There is no right or wrong answer so be clear in the reasoning behind your decisions
Interview	As above	
Group discussion	The group will be given a mini case-study or task and are expected to prepare a response collectively	Listen to points made by other candidates. Make clear and constructive contributions to the discussion. Read between the lines to find out what is implied but not stated

brilliant dos and don'ts

Do

✔ Have realistic expectations of when they are going to let you know if you have been successful. If they haven't got back to you in a week then you could call them to enquire; this shows you are still interested and keen. If they haven't got back to you within a day, this is too early to call and probably won't go down very well with the company. You can always ask at the interview when you would expect to hear.

✔ Evaluate your performance – what you think went well and what didn't go so well – in an honest way. If you get the job you will have done some valuable self-assessment, which is key to career progression. If you don't get the job, then you will be able to highlight your weaker areas and work on these for next time. Ask the employer for feedback, whichever way the result goes, as this is vital for your own development.

Don't

✗ Count your chickens: even if the interview went well you may not be the right candidate or they may have someone who has more experience they want to employ instead. Even if this is the job you really want, continue to apply for other roles and attend any other interviews. If you don't get this one, then you still have other prospects!

Claire Thomas, Graduate Marketing Manager, Centrica

Do

✔ Ask for feedback if you have been unsuccessful in order that you can learn for next time.

✔ Follow up with the organisation if you have not heard anything in the time they had specified.

Don't

✗ Give up if you are not successful first time – there is more than one way to access opportunities in an organisation.

Helen Alkin, Recruitment Manager, Marks and Spencer plc

 recap

● Use your careers service.

● Identify how your existing skills translate into skills valued by employers.

● Identify any skills gaps and create an action plan to develop these skills.

● Preparation is central to all elements of the selection process.

● Research the company, the industry and their competitors.

● Think of relevant examples to selection criteria drawn from both academic and non-academic activities.

● Use STAR to structure your answers.

● Remember that communication is both verbal and non-verbal.

● Always remember, you only get one chance to create a first impression, so make it a good one!

CHAPTER 7

A Brilliant future

To believe in your brilliance is to
remove any limitations from your
future

T o ensure a Brilliant future you really need to understand what employability means to potential employers, your degree discipline and more importantly to you. Despite the fact that both employers and universities make provision for the development of employability skills through the curriculum through the availability of work experience, respectively, ultimately the key driver of your development of employability skills is you. You will determine your level of engagement and to what degree you get involved. As a result it is important to fully understand the 'I' in the I Brand Employability Model (see p. 72) as, despite all the opportunities available, students' experiences will vary in relation to their levels of effort and involvement. This further emphasises the importance of your 'individual brand' as everyone will be different: students will differ in the priority they give to developing employability skills and their interpretation of what employability means to them.

Why is employability important?

The changes in the higher education sector will continually increase the importance of employability not only for students, but will also place the onus on universities to ensure they are producing graduates who can 'hit the ground running'. The increase in fees will raise students' expectations from their institution to ensure 'success' upon graduation. Success will be defined in terms of their ability to secure employment, especially with the expectation that they will become liable to repay tuition fees once their salaries surpass £21,000. Currently universities are required to produce a public statement outlining how they promote employability to students and, by 2012, students will be able to see the employment statistics for each course and so make informed decisions about not only where to study, but also which course.

Employers also place heavy emphasis on employability skills, as, although they recognise their role in the development of graduates, they also see the importance of graduates harnessing and developing their own skills. This shows drive and ingenuity, which will always be valued in any sector. Students who are able to practically demonstrate and draw on examples that show their understanding of generic employability skills will advance far quicker in the graduate market. Do remember that employability does not guarantee employment, but definitely enhances the prospects of graduates to secure employment. The statistics highlighted in 'The graduate market' (High Fliers Research, 2011) emphasised the fact that a third of all graduate vacancies in 2011 will go to graduates who have previously worked at the organisation and students with no work experience will struggle to secure a graduate role.

Employability will continue to increase in importance and universities, employers and students will place more emphasis on developing ways to attain these skills while at university. As stated above, a number of universities have employability awards that both recognise and encourage students to engage with extra-curricular activities. Employers have also developed schemes to circumvent the introduction of fees to maintain access levels for a wider selection of students from all backgrounds who may (due to the increase in fees) have discounted the idea of attending university.

What is employability?

Mantze Yorke (2006a) defines employability as:

'a set of achievements – skills, understanding and personal attributes – that makes graduates more likely to gain employment and be successful in their chosen occupations, which benefits themselves, the workforce, the community and the economy.'

Graduate employers recognise a range of generic employability skills that underpin the ability of a graduate to perform in the workplace. The I Brand Employability Model (reproduced on overleaf for reference) recognises the skills embedded within your course, but also the need to develop practical examples of generic employability skills drawn from your extra-curricular activities, work experience or voluntary work.

The 'I' in the model recognises your individual effort and contribution. The model acknowledges that students' background and personality will influence how they engage with employability both within their course and extra-curricular activities. As mentioned, networking is a key factor in gaining employment and identifying opportunities. The extended network of students is dependent upon their background and their ability to widen their network via their parents' associations and business contacts. This can create a significant disparity in opportunities available to students, as it is dependent not on ability but the social and economic standing of your parents. Your ability to recognise opportunities and take calculated risks is part of your personal make-up and so I Enterprise recognises a students' ability to add value through innovative and creative approaches to tasks. Enterprising skills are highly valued among employers. I Marketing draws heavily on the analogy of marketing a product and encourages students to review all aspects of their marketing strategy. How will they promote their product in the marketplace? How will they stand out?

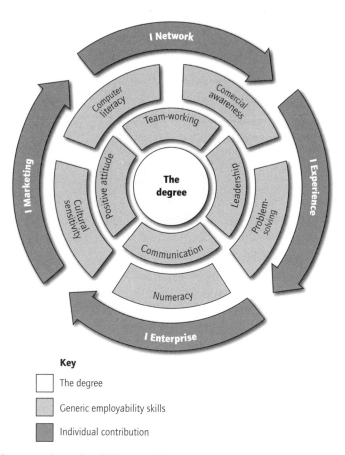

Key

The degree

Generic employability skills

Individual contribution

The I Brand Employability Model

This is an important aspect of the model as students need to understand their strengths and weaknesses – essentially, their unique selling point – in order to communicate this factor to potential employers. Every student should be able to answer the question 'Why would an employer choose me over another graduate?'

The I Experience highlights and emphasises the different backgrounds, cultural differences and motivational drivers for each student. Student experience is unique and personal to each student, so it is important to recognise this factor when developing employability skills. Students bring their 'personal baggage' to the table and ultimately it will impact their engagement and development of employability skills.

Whose responsibility is it?

Ultimately the responsibility rests with the student. Universities clearly have a role to play in ensuring students are provided with opportunities to develop employability skills within the curriculum and through the provision of extra-curricular activities. Employers have a responsibility to ensure the provision of varied work experience opportunities. In the end it all comes back to the students' willingness to partake in these opportunities. Each student's level of engagement will vary.

What opportunities exist to develop employability skills?

Employability is embedded into the curriculum. Through various methods of assessment, students are given the opportunity to develop a range of skills. The key issue is the fact that these opportunities are seldom labelled as such and so few students actually connect the dots and recognise the transferable nature of the skills they develop on their courses and their relevance to the world of work. Vital skills are learnt and honed during assessment, which will not only develop essential skills for the workplace but also for the interview process to secure a graduate role. The table overleaf (reproduced from Chapter 1) reinforces the connection between assessment methods and the skills required in the workplace.

The other avenue for developing employability skills is through extra-curricular activities. Both on and off campus, students have the opportunity to develop skills through involvement with the student's union or undertaking internships or voluntary work. It is through this practical application and demonstration of employability skills that students enhance their ability to stand

Assessment method	Transferable skills
Group assignments	Students are often required to work in teams to complete a group task. Students develop project management, team-building, negotiation and influencing skills, all highly relevant to the world of work
Presentations	The ability to develop a well-structured presentation that communicates the key points effectively and efficiently is a valuable skill, useful in a variety of situations beyond a degree
Case-study analysis	The case-study analysis presents a business scenario and requires students to utilise critical thinking, analytical and problem-solving skills not only to identify the key challenges but also make recommendations drawing on both the internal and external environment faced by the organisation. Case-studies are often used within the selection process to differentiate candidates
Report-writing	Accuracy and clarity in report-writing is a must! Literacy skills are central to your academic studies and for application forms and writing reports or emails in the workplace
Problem-based learning	The ability to resolve problems and provide well-founded solutions is directly transferable to the workplace, where students will be continually presented with challenges
Research	Research skills are applicable to all industries. The ability to collate, synthesise, analyse and clearly present information found can add value to all organisations, whether private, public or third-sector. All industries are reliant upon information to provide insights into current industry dynamics, future trends and possible opportunities and threats in the marketplace
Personal development planning (PDP)	PDP encourages reflection on your strengths and weaknesses and develops self-awareness, which supports your continual development and learning
Examinations	Examinations present the opportunity to apply your understanding to scenarios or questions within a time constraint. Many professions utilise professional examinations to test candidates' knowledge and application of the subject matter. An ability to pass examinations is a required skill within the work environment. Examinations are also used as part of the interview process and so have relevance in many work-related situations

out. These activities not only enrich the student experience but also provide a wealth of examples that students can draw on in an interview or selection process. Once again it relies on the students' ability to both recognise and connect the skills they are developing to the generic employability skills valued by graduate recruiters. Below is a recap of some of the skills that can be developed through extra-curricular activity and how they relate to the world of work.

● Leadership skills
  – You don't have to be the president of a society to develop leadership skills. Taking ownership of a task or role and demonstrating the ability to influence, negotiate for resources and motivate others to achieve a common goal are all examples of leadership qualities. These skills will resonate with an employer, as one of an organisation's goals is to identify people who have the ability to lead/manage a team.

● Project management
  – Whether you are at university or in the workplace, you will always need to have a clear plan of action of how you will achieve your goals. The ability to plan, adhere to deadlines and identify key milestones to succeed are all part of the organisational skills required within the work environment.

● Event management
  – The co-ordination and planning involved in organising a successful event demonstrate your ability to multitask and strong organisational skills. Event management requires a high level of organisational skills, from liaising with speakers and developing and distributing the marketing communication to negotiating additional resources. The ability to co-ordinate a successful event is an impressive addition to your CV. The busy workplace will always

require the ability to multitask while maintaining standards. Organisational skills and the ability to meet deadlines are musts for successful graduates.

● Budgeting

   – The ability to budget and forecast demonstrates an understanding of how decisions will affect the bottom line. For instance, understanding how to budget for the costs associated with an event and balance these costs in relation to ticket sales to break even and or make a profit are valuable skills. All organisations will value these skills and will especially value your ability to highlight the relationship between decision-making and the impact on costs, as the economy requires all industries to operate efficiently. These skills are directly transferable to all industry sectors.

● Communication

   – Both written and spoken communication can be developed by participating in a university society and their value is transferable to the workplace. The ability to write a persuasive email or report requesting support for the society or the development of effective marketing materials providing members with updates and information are useful skills. Employers will expect a high standard of literacy and communication skills. You will be required to produce reports, communicate with clients and provide information to other departments in the organisation.

● Networking

   – Networking will help the enterprising student secure additional resources for his or her society and generally meet individuals from different backgrounds and interests. Networking is the backbone of all business. The ability to maintain a wide network is useful not only for university but also identifying possible opportunities.

Employability is a continual process. This is reinforced by the circular nature of the model. While at university and beyond you will continue to develop your employability skills and also redefine which skills are important to you and prospective employers.

Are there jobs out there and can I have one?

Good question. When all is said and done and students have done all they can to develop employability skills, will they be rewarded with a graduate role? The graduate opportunities in 2011 are on the rise and the outlook is more promising, but students cannot afford to be complacent. Companies have raised the stakes and many require an upper second as the minimum for entry to their graduate schemes. More than a third of all graduate vacancies will go to students who have previously undertaken work experience with the companies concerned. As a result, students need to understand the importance of not only developing employability skills but also establishing links with companies during their studies.

Work experience has become a vital ingredient in a graduate's ability to secure employment. As a result, 63 per cent of the top graduate recruiters offer work experience opportunities for graduates in the form of both internships and placements. The competition for these positions is fierce and students will have to undergo a series of selection processes in order to be successful.

When I grow up I want to be a ...?

Choosing the right career is often one of the most difficult decisions for students. How do you know you will like your chosen career path? Knowing you will be the best starting point! Having a good understanding of what motivates you and what is a priority for you in the workplace will help you not only identify suitable roles but also suitable companies. This can be supported by undertaking research into possible career options, both discipline-related and unrelated. There are many successful professionals who have not taken the automatic career path for their degree discipline. Learning from the experiences of alumni is also another option. Alumni can provide insight into career options and their own experience of the working world. Regardless of your discipline, there will be various roles available to you and it is always useful to speak with professionals in these roles to find out whether the role is suitable for you. Internships and placements also give you a different perspective about a role; there is no substitute for work experience to provide a behind-the-scenes look at possible career options.

This can be easier said than done. Finding work experience and ultimately a graduate position is not an easy feat. An internship provides you with the opportunity to see if a career is for you, but also provides an employer with the opportunity to test-drive your product. If you are not fortunate enough to find an internship there are other ways to gain work experience. Temporary roles or job shadowing are also methods of gaining a practical insight into a potential career choice.

Communicating your Brilliance

As highlighted above, the ability to translate your employability skills into those valued by employers is an art in itself. Identifying your strengths and weaknesses and areas for development are all essential when trying to find both work experience and graduate roles. The ability to communicate your Brilliance will rely heavily on your verbal and literacy skills and your ability to present yourself both physically and on paper in a manner acceptable to employers. Preparation is central to all of the elements of the selection process, from writing your CV to attending your first interview. Your success will be underpinned by planning, researching the company and the role, reflecting upon your experiences and identifying how they match the selection criteria.

Using the STAR framework – Situation, Task, Action, Result – to review your work experience, tasks undertaken on your course and your extra-curricular activities will help you to match your skill set to the requirements of your employers. You will be surprised at how many examples you will be able to draw upon.

Being meticulous in your preparation in all stages of the selection process is paramount. An error on your CV or arriving late for an interview speaks volumes about your character and creates a bad impression. If you cannot manage yourself, how will you manage any of the clients' business relationships or processes? Researching the company and having knowledge of their main competitors, the challenges they face in the marketplace and a general understanding of the business environment will support you in your interview and add value to your responses. Employers will be impressed if you take the time to find out not only about their company but also any challenges faced by the organisation. Prepare, prepare, prepare, as it can make the difference between a successful application and being overlooked in favour of another candidate.

A continuous Career Life Cycle

Employability is not an end in itself. Once you begin your career, then you need to continually reflect upon your employability skills to ensure your skills are still aligned with the needs of your employer and your industry sector. For instance, IT is continually changing and influencing sector development. Social media has had an impact on all sectors in some way, with companies utilising social networks both informally and formally. You can't afford to stand still now that you have secured a graduate position, as life is constantly moving!

As you develop, mature and move through your Career Life Cycle, your needs and wants will also change. What you defined as career goals and ambitions may change as you get older or your circumstances change.

The circular nature of the I Brand Employability Model emphasises the continuous process of employability. You will continue to grow and develop and this in turn will inform your employability. Your degree is a three- or four-year course and throughout that time you will be exposed to many different experiences that will influence the direction of your future career. University is a time to explore, research and investigate various career options and the skills required. There are also many opportunities to build and develop your network, both within and external to your university, so don't miss out!

The need to be determined in your search of a career is paramount. Building your employability skills while at university is not an option but a necessity. You cannot afford to ignore your employability until after graduation. Start building and developing your employability skills from day one to get ahead of the game!

 **recap**

- Make sure you understand what employability means for your discipline and potential graduate recruiters.

- You determine to what degree you engage with developing employability skills.

- The success of a university is strongly linked to the ability of its graduates to secure graduate employment.

- Ultimately the responsibility of developing employability skills rests with the students, as they have to make an active decision to engage.

- Students need to recognise the opportunties embedded within

▶

their courses to develop transferable skills relevant to the workplace.

- Extra-curricular activities provide students with the opportunity to give practical demonstrations of their employability skills in action.

- Leadership skills, project mangement skills, event management, budgeting and communication are all skills that can be developed through extra-curricular activities.

- Employability is a continual process and each stage of your career will require you to redefine the skills you need to develop in order to progress.

- Take every possible opportunity to network and develop links with companies while studying.

- Take time to explore both discipline-related and non-discipline-related career options.

- Try to gain work experience in your chosen field: this is a good test to see if this career is for you.

- Be meticulous in your preparation at all stages in the application process.

- Employability is not an optional extra – place it at the heart of your university experience.

Useful resources

Further reading

Hodgson, S. (2008) *Brilliant Answers to Tough Interview Questions*. Pearson Education.

Jay, R. (2007) *Brilliant Interviews: What employers want to hear and how to say it*. Pearson Education.

McIvor, B. (2008) *Career Detection: Finding and managing your career*. Management Briefs.

Norton, Tom, and Thomas, Hayley (2009) 'Beyond the curriculum: Opportunities to enhance employability and future life choices'. Policy report, the 1994 Group's Student Experience Policy Group. www.1994group.ac.uk/documents/public/Publications/BeyondTheCurriculum_Nov09.pdf (accessed June 2011).

Southon, M. (2010) *This is How Yoodoo It*. Ecademy Press.

Yorke, M. (2006b) *Embedding Employability into the Curriculum*. Higher Education Academy, Enhancing Student Employability Co-ordination Team.

Useful websites

Association of Graduate Recruiters www.agr.org.uk

British Universities & Colleges Sport www.bucs.org.uk

Do-it.org www.do-it.org.uk

The Duke of Edinburgh's Award www.dofe.org

Graduate Talent Pool http://graduatetalentpool.direct.gov.uk

High Fliers Research Ltd www.highfliers.co.uk

Higher Education Careers Services Unit www.hecsu.ac.uk

Inspiring Interns www.inspiringinterns.com

National Council for Graduate Entrepreneurship
www.ncge.org.uk

Prospects www.prospects.ac.uk

Rare Recruitment www.rarerecruitment.co.uk

Rate My Placement.com www.ratemyplacement.co.uk

SHL www.shl.com/TryATest

Mike Southon www.mikesouthon.com

Students In Free Enterprise www.sife.org

Target Jobs www.targetjobs.co.uk

Young Enterprise Scheme www.young-enterprise.org.uk

References

AGCAS (2011) 'Employability: An AGCAS position statement.' http://agcas.org.uk/assets/download?file=2262&parent=725. (accessed June 2011).

Association of Graduate Recruiters (AGR) (2010) www.agr. org.uk/Content/Class-of-2010-Faces-Uphill-Struggle-for-Jobs (accessed June 2011).

Association of Graduate Recruiters (AGR) (2011a) www.agr. org.uk/Content/Brighter-outlook-for-graduates-as-vacancy-numbers-increase-for-first-time-since-recession-began (accessed June 2011).

Association of Graduate Recruiters (AGR) (2011b) 'Graduate recruitment survey 2011 – winter review'. www.agr.org.uk

Browne, Lord John (2010) 'Securing a sustainable future for higher education: An independent review of higher education funding & student finance' Government paper. www. independent.gov.uk/browne-report (accessed June 2011).

CBI (2009) 'Future fit: Preparing graduates for the world of Work'. www.cbi.org.uk/pdf/20090326-CBI-FutureFit-Preparing-graduates-for-the-world-of-work.pdf (accessed June 2011).

CBI/EDI (2010) 'Ready to grow: Business priorities for education and skills: Education and Skills Survey 2010.' www.cbi. org.uk/pdf/20100501-cbi-education-and-skills-survey-2010.pdf (accessed June 2011).

Dearing, Sir Ron (1997) 'The reports of the National Committee of Inquiry into Higher Education' (the Dearing report). www.leeds.ac.uk/educol/ncihe/nr_007.htm. (accessed June 2011).

High Fliers Research (2011) 'The graduate market in 2011 www.highfliers.co.uk/download/GMReport11.pdf (accessed June 2011).

Jones, D. Foreword, Prospects Directory. Prospects. (2004)

Kotler, P., Armstrong, G., Wong, V. and Saunders, J. (2008) *Principles of Marketing*, 5th Edition. Pearson Education.

Karinthy, F. (1929) 'Chains' in *Everything is Different*. (out of print).

Maher, A. and Graves, S. (2008) *Graduate Employability: Can higher education deliver?* Threshold Press.

McNair, S. (2003) *Employability in Higher Education*. LTSN Generic Centre/University of Surrey.

Mokades, R. (2011) *Three Steps to Success*. Profile Books.

Rene, C. *The Students' Guide to Networking*. (unpublished work).

Robbins, L. (1963) 'Higher education report to the committee appointed by the Prime Minister under the chairmanship of Lord Robbins, 1961–1963' HMSO. Chapter 2, paragraph 25, p. 6.

Scherer, A. (2011) *Brilliant Intern*. Prentice Hall.

Peacock, Lousia (2010) 'Best and worst universities for graduate jobs', *The Telegraph*, 29 July. www.telegraph.co.uk/finance/jobs/8138447/Best-and-worst-universities-for-graduate-jobs.html (accessed 4 April 2011).

Collins, Nick (2010) 'Up to one in four graduates faces unemployment', *The Telegraph*, 16 July. www.telegraph.co.uk/education/universityeducation/7892235/Up-to-one-in-four-graduates-faces-unemployment.html. (accessed 3 April 2011).

Willets, D. (2010) House of Commons debate, 8 July 2010, Column 511, *Daily Hansard – Debate.* www.publications.parliament.uk/pa/cm201011/cmhansrd/cm100708/debtext/100708-0001.htm (accessed June 2011).

Yorke, M. (2006a) *Learning and Skills Series One: Employability: What it is and what it is not.* Higher Education Academy, Enhancing Student Employability Co-ordination Team.

APPENDIX

I Brand worksheets

What is employability?

Below is a list of employability skills valued by employers. At the beginning of the academic year rate yourself on how well you have developed these skills. Rate yourself out of 5, with 1 being 'very well' and 5 representing 'needs development'.

	1	2	3	4	5
Computer literacy					
Cultural sensitivity					
Commercial awareness					
Team-working					
Problem-solving					
Numeracy					
Positive attitude					
Communication					
Leadership					

Review your degree programme and highlight any degree-specific employability skills.

	1	2	3	4	5

If you have scored 3 or below, develop an action plan to further develop these skills (see overleaf).

Action plan

Skill	Why are these skills important?	Action to be taken (show how you will develop the skill)	How will you demonstrate your skill?	Date for completion
Example: team-work	In the workplace you will be required to work in teams	Join student society or sports team	Take on a specific function in order to draw on examples of specific actions taken	End of academic year

Your degree

Employability is embedded in your degree programme. Make a list below of the units for each term and identify the employability skills you are developing. Review the assessment methods, current industry/sector information, guest speakers, etc.

Subject	Employability skills

Review the feedback on your assignments and reflect upon your self-management when completing the tasks. What did you do well and what areas need further development? Consider, for example, how you managed your time, interacted with others, how well you researched the topic, etc. Now use the table below to identify the top three areas to focus on in the following semester.

Area for development	Outline how you will develop this skill and by when

Use the STAR (Situation Task, Action, Result) matrix below to develop these examples into possible answers for application forms.

Skill	Situation (outline the situation)	Task (define the task)	Action (what action did you take?)	Result (what was the outcome?)
Leadership				
Team-work				
Communication				
Postitive attitude				
Problem- solving				

Continuous use of this framework will enable you not only to review your development of employability skills but also your ability to relate examples drawn from your degree to skills valued by employers.

Freshers' fair checklist

A freshers' fair is usually held at the start of the academic year to provide new students with the opportunity to find out about the students' union, clubs and societies and other extra-curricular activities.

Who is the president of the students' union? Make a note of name and contact details

Make a list of all the societies at the university which are of interest

Make a note of the societies' contact details and the date of the next meeting.

What other extra-curricular activities are available at the university?

Make a list of other activities you might want to join. Note their contact details

If you are interested in starting your own society, email the president of the students' union to find out how

Is there a society related to your specific discipline? If yes, join. If not, this is a perfect opportunity to start a new society!

Voluntary work and you

Assess your availability and identify possible volunteering opportunities. Create a timetable that highlights your lecture and study times, your part-time job, society meeting times and the days and time you would be willing to volunteer. Remember you can volunteer in your holidays and so it does not need to conflict with your schedule at university.

	Monday	Tuesday	Wednesday	Thursday	Friday	Saturday	Sunday
9.00							
10.00							
11.00							
12.00							
13.00							
14.00							
15.00							
16.00							
17.00							
18.00							
19.00							

Websites to search for volunteering opportunities:

www.do-it.org

www.volunteering.org.uk

Your university careers service.

The graduate market and your industry/sector

Questions

1   Ask your course director or careers service for the statistics on destinations of leavers from your course.

2   Which employers have recruited from your course in previous years?

3   For what roles are students from your course typically recruited?

4   Did students in previous years undertake internships and placements? If so where and for whom?

5   Review 'The Graduate Market in 2011' by High Fliers Research (2011). What are the graduate recruitment statistics for your sector?

6   Ask your course director if it would be possible to speak with the alumni of your course to gain from their experiences following graduation.

7   Identify sector-specific magazines or journals to keep you abreast of changes in the sector.

8   Find the professional body that represents your sector:
    – name
    – contact details
    – student subscription fee
    – networking events
    – sign up for e-bulletin.

Start your own business

1 What business support is offered at your university?
   - Name
   - Contact details
   - Enterprise training
   - Grants and funding

2 Is there a student enterprise society?
   - Name
   - Contact details
   - Meeting times

3 Does your university operate a small business incubator unit? What support does the unit offer to current students?
   - Contact name
   - Contact details
   - Location

4 Is the university involved in any enterprise competitions?
   - Name
   - Details of the competition
   - Entry requirements
   - Closing date.

Part-time job review

Whether you are stacking shelves or frying burgers, you are developing your employability skills. This exercise will help you to translate your part-time skills development into skills valued by a graduate employer.

Job title:

_____

Outline the key functions of your role:

_____

How does your function contribute to the overall success of the company?

_____

If your role disappeared tomorrow, what impact would this have on customers' experience?

_____

_____

How do you think your skills could be considered in a wider context in relation to:

customer service

_____

leadership

_____

project management

_____

organisational skills

_____ ▶

team-working

problem-solving

communication

Use the STAR (Situation, Task, Action, Result) matrix to review and demonstrate some of the skills outlined above.

Skill	Situation (outline the situation)	Task (define the task)	Action (what action did you take?)	Result (what was the outcome?)
Leadership				
Team-work				
Communication				
Postitive attitude				
Problem-solving				

Getting to know you

Conduct a personal review of yourself and distribute it to at least five others who know you in differing capacities: lecturer, colleague, fellow student, etc. Your personal review will provide an insight into your strengths and areas for development.

1 = very good   5 = needs development

Traits and skills valued by employers	1	2	3	4	5
Punctual					
Reliable					
Attention to detail					
Problem-solving					
Communication (oral and written)					
Numerate					
Innovative					
Positive attitude					
Honest					
Meet deadlines					
Accurate					
Can think on your feet					
Organised					
Team player					
Leader					
Negotiator					
Influencer					
Name one strength					
Name one area for development					

Employability workshops available on campus

You should attend these free workshops at your university, which are often run by the careers service. Throughout your degree and as you progress in the development of your employability skills, you will need to revisit previously attended workshops and your needs and wants will change. The process of applying for an internship, placement or graduate role are very competitive and these workshops can help you review what you have to offer a potential employer.

Workshop	Date booked	Location
Application forms		
Developing a CV		
Covering letters		
Interview skills		
Assessment centres		
Psychometric testing		
Job-hunting skills		
Communication skills		
Assertiveness in the workplace		
Leadership skills		

Your individual brand

What does your brand say about you?

Write a short statement (no more than 100 words) that captures your unique selling point: what makes you stand out? This statement should capture the skills developed on your degree and through your extra-curricular activities. You should also capture your 'I', your individual contribution to tasks – what you bring to the table as a team member, leader and project manager.

Continually revisit this statement, incorporating your new skills. Compare your statement from year one to your statement in your final year.

Personal statement: year one

Personal statement: year two

Personal statement: year three

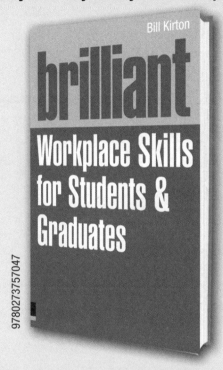

...nt at University

Get started on your graduate career

Judith Done & Rachel Mulvey

brilliant

Graduate Career Handbook

9780273744887

Brilliant Graduate Career Handbook gives you the help and
information you need to get started on your graduate career
– what's out there, how to make sense of it, and how to make
good choices.

Brilliant Outcomes:

✓ Understand the labour market and how to navigate it

✓ Begin to decide what to do with your degree once you have graduated

✓ Learn how to make the best use of opportunities around to develop your
skills and experience for the future

Prentice Hall

Available fr...   ...ps